The motte and keep at Sandal

THE CASTLES
AND TOWER HOUSES
OF YORKSHIRE

Mike Salter

FOLLY PUBLICATIONS

ACKNOWLEDGEMENTS

Most of the photographs in this book were taken by the author, and a number of old postcards from his collection have also been reproduced. The author also drew the plans and the map. Plans are to common scales of 1:400 for keeps, towers and gatehouses, 1:800 for courtyard buildings, 1:2000 and 1:10000 for site plans of large buildings and earthworks. Peter Ryder supplied the photos of Ayton, Hellifield, Kilton, Kirkby Moorside, Markenfield, Mortham, Mulgrave, Riccal, Steeton, Temple Hirst and Upsall. He also made available a lot of other material, on which several of the plans are based. The author is greatly indebted to Peter, and also to Helen Thomas for driving on fieldwork trips, and to Marjorie Salter for proof reading.

AUTHOR'S NOTES

This series of books (see full list inside back cover) are intended as portable field guides giving as much information and illustrative material as possible in volumes of modest size, weight and price. As a whole the series gives a lot of information on lesser known sites about which little information has tended to appear in print. The aim in the castle books has been to mention, where the information is known to the author, owners or custodians of buildings who erected or altered parts of them, and those who were the first or last to hold an estate, an important office, or a title. Those in occupation at the time of dramatic events such as sieges or royal visits are also often named. Other owners and occupants whose lives had little effect on the condition of the buildings are not generally mentioned, nor are most 19th and 20th century events, unless particularly dramatic, nor ghost stories or legends.

The books are intended to be used in conjunction with the Ordnance Survey 1:50,000 maps. Grid references are given in the gazetteers together with a coding system indicating which buildings can be visited or easily seen by the public which is explained on page 13. Generally speaking, maps will be required to find most of the lesser known sites, the majority of which are not regularly open to the public.

Each level of a building is called a storey in this book, the basement being the first or lowest storey with its floor near courtyard level unless mentioned as otherwise.

Measurements given in the text and scales on the plans are given in metres, the unit used by the author for all measurements taken on site. Although the buildings were designed using feet and inches the metric scales are much easier to use and are now standard amongst those studying historic buildings and ancient sites. For those who feel a need to make a conversion 3 metres is almost 10 feet. Unless specifically mentioned as otherwise all dimensions are external at or near ground level, but above the plinth if there is one. On plans the original work is shown black, post-1800 work is stippled, and alterations and additions of intermediate periods are hatched.

ABOUT THE AUTHOR

Mike Salter is 48 and has been a professional writer and publisher since he went on the Government Enterprise Allowance Scheme for unemployed people in 1988. He is particularly interested in the planning and layout of medieval buildings and has a huge collection of plans of castles and churches he has measured during tours (mostly by bicycle and motorcycle) throughout all parts of the British Isles since 1968. Wolverhampton born and bred, Mike now lives in an old cottage beside the Malvern Hills. His other interests include walking, maps, railways, board games, morris dancing, playing percussion instruments and calling dances with a folk group.

First published December 2001. Copyright Mike Salter.
Folly Publications, Folly Cottage, 151 West Malvern Rd, Malvern, Worcs WR14 4AY
Printed by Aspect Design, 89 Newtown Rd, Malvern, Worcs WR14 2PD

Gateway arch with portcullis groove at Ravensworth

CONTENTS

A map of sites described appears inside the front cover.

INTRODUCTION

The story of castles in Yorkshire begins with the invasion of England by William, Duke of Normandy in 1066. During his twenty year reign as King of England William founded many castles the earliest ones in Yorkshire being the two standing on either side of the River Ouse erected in 1068 and 1069 to keep the city in check. William gave estates to his chief followers in return for specified periods of military service, and the new lords gave units of land called manors to their knights also in return for military service, which often included garrison duty, this system being called feudalism and an innovation in England. The thin veneer of landowning and French-speaking Normans thus consolidated their fragile hold over the Saxon populace by constructing castles serving as residences, strongholds and as symbols of rank. The Romans, Saxons and Vikings all built forts and defences around settlements, as at York itself, but the Normans introduced the idea of powerful individuals erecting fortresses to serve as residences and as the administrative centres of groups of manors. The Domesday Book survey commissioned by King William in 1986 to record who was holding what land and what it was considered to be worth records a number of castles in Yorkshire, and also records the terrible destruction that William had wreaked in the north to stamp out resistance, many districts then still lying waste. With one exception these castles were not of mortared stone but of earth and wood, materials which allowed a more rapid construction and some prefabrication.

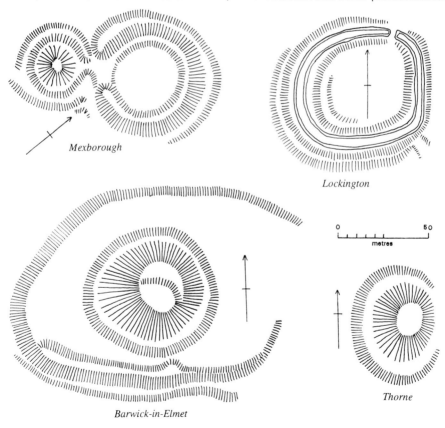

Mexborough

Lockington

0   50
metres

Barwick-in-Elmet

Thorne

Plans of Norman Castle Earthworks

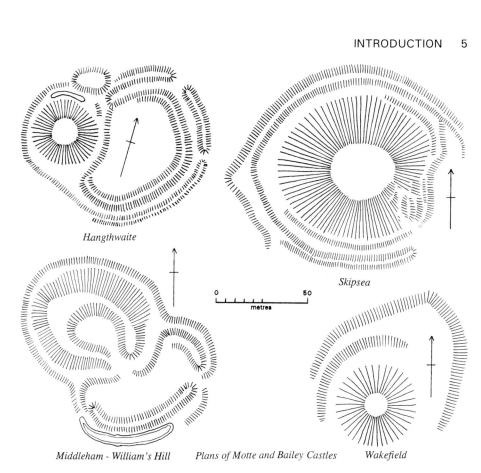

Hangthwaite

Skipsea

0   50
metres

Middleham - William's Hill   Plans of Motte and Bailey Castles   Wakefield

Castles built in the late 11th century often had a high mound raised from material taken out of the surrounding ditch and having on top the lord's residence in the form of a two or three storey timber-framed tower surrounded by a palisade. The mound summit was reached by a ramp up from a forecourt or bailey in which were sited a range of stores, workshops, a hall and other apartments, and a chapel, all originally built of wood. Sometimes the mound took an alternative form known to modern writers as a ringwork, with a high rampart surrounding the lord's house, and the greater castles usually had an additional outer bailey beyond the main entrance. Castles of these types continued to be built for over a century after the Norman Conquest and can only be precisely dated when there is a historical record of their foundation or good archaeological evidence, both of which are lacking for many of the earthwork sites described in this book. The most impressive castles were the headquarters of great lords, but there were many smaller castles built by their followers, who owed annual military service at the greater castles. The basic design varied according to the terrain and resources available. Baileys and other outworks were omitted or duplicated and made whatever size and shape local circumstances dictated. Natural landscape features were used where possible, hillocks and spurs being shaped and heightened into steep-sided and level topped mottes, whilst one of the two castles at York was protected a combination of wet moats and a lake provided by damming up an adjacent river. The double ditch system at Helmsley is thought to be a symbol of regality, the builder being a step-brother of the king.

Arch in the keep at Richmond

Scolland's Hall, Richmond

Pickering: Plan of keep

For the first two generations after the Norman invasion of 1066 masons were in short supply compared with carpenters and labourers, partly because the Saxons and Danes mostly erected buildings of wood except for the most important churches. Buildings of mortared stone took several years of comparatively peaceful conditions to construct. Fortifications would have been vulnerable to attack during the long periods when foundations were being laid so structures raised quickly on timber posts were seen as an easier option when defences were required in a hurry. Timber buildings were vulnerable to accidental or deliberate destruction by fire and eventually rotted away when in constant contact with damp soil. Although structures of wood remained an important element in the defences of most castles up until the 14th century, the most important parts of the defences and the chief domestic buildings within them would be gradually replaced with structures of mortared stone.

Most of the stonework to be seen in Yorkshire castles dates from the mid 12th century onwards, and the castle at York itself was not rebuilt in stone until the mid 13th century but there is one spectacular earlier building, Richmond, which dates probably from the 1070s. Perched on a rocky site that was good for defence but less conveniently located for administrative purposes, it comprised a stone curtain wall around a triangular court with several small towers on the side least well defended by nature and three gateways, one of which was a substantial rectangular tower. It also had a stone hall block. In Britain the only other 11th century castles with stone enclosures are Rochester, Chepstow and Ludlow. In Yorkshire the only other stonework likely to be earlier than the 1150s is the early 12th century curtain wall and square gatehouse at Tickhill, and perhaps the old hall at Pickering.

After the chaos of the civil war during King Stephen's reign (1135-54) the Crown attempted to exercise greater control over possession of castles, which in effect controlled the land. The construction of embattled secular buildings was regulated and from the 1190s the Crown issued licences to crenellate (embattle) the dwellings of barons who were considered trustworthy. Henry II (1154-89) enforced the surrender of castles held by suspect barons. Some of them were destroyed and others retained as royal strongholds. In the 1160s Henry built a new keep and curtain wall at Scarborough, one of the baronial castles he had taken over. This keep was a tall square building of three storeys containing a hall over a basement and two private rooms on the top level, with the walls then rising high above the roof and originally having corner turrets. It was entered at hall level through a forebuilding, the upper storey of which contained a chapel. A similar structure was erected by the Earl of Richmond at Richmond during the 1160s, and an outer court was added probably whilst the castle was in royal hands during the 1170s. The Earl of Richmond's other keep at Bowes was designed on different lines. This was a hall keep of just two storeys with the hall and private chamber side-by-side on the upper level. A second keep of this type dating from the 1160s or 70s at Middleham is large enough to contain three rooms on the upper storey, the extra room being a presence chamber where the lord would receive guests and sit in judgment on the affairs of his estate.

Square towers have blind corners that are vulnerable to undermining and were eventually superseded by circular and polygonal towers, although the latter are not very common. Circular towers became the norm in the 13th century but the North of England remained conservative and in the 14th century reverted to building rectangular towers which were more convenient for habitation. Yorkshire contained two keeps dating from Henry II's reign of the type known as transitional, when polygonal and circular forms were first experimented with. Only the foundations remain of an eleven-sided tower built by the king himself on the motte at Tickhill, but the superb circular tower keep built by his half-brother probably in the 1180s at Conisborough remains almost complete and has recently been given a new roof and upper floors. Although slightly smaller than that at Tickhill the Conisborough keep was the taller and more impressive of the two, with the unique feature of six evenly-spaced buttresses around it. They are solid all the way to the top except that a delightful vaulted chapel is created in one of them, opening off the uppermost of two private rooms forming the third and fourth storeys. Of about the same period is the bailey curtain wall which is flanked by small solid circular turrets. The very damaged and overgrown castles of Mulgrave and Kilton both have work of the early 13th century, although parts of Kilton may go back to the 1160s.

Chapel at Pontefract

The wall of the inner bailey at Pickering dating from the 1180s abuts a slightly earlier hall block. This castle has yet another type of keep known to modern writers as a shell keep in which the palisade around the summit of a motte was replaced by a stone wall forming a small enclosure with detached or lean-to buildings inside. Such a keep probably existed at Pickering by the 1180s but the existing fragmentary structure is a rebuild of the 1220s, when the a new hall and chapel were also erected. The unusually massive curtain wall with several square towers at Pontefract is also thought to be late 12th century and three of the gatehouses on the circuit of the city walls at York are also of that period, although the walls themselves are later.

King John (1199-1216) spent a fortune refortifying the castles of Knaresborough and Scarborough. At Knaresborough the only relic of his period is the great ditch, but Scarborough has a very long wall cutting off the landward side of the headland. The round towers of the earliest section (pre 1206) are solid and of slight projection, but those of the second campaign are more advanced D-shaped structures containing two storeys of rooms with arrow-loops in deep embrasures. There are also remains of an aisled hall and a separate chamber block of that period. The castle built at Helmsley c1200-20 was of an advanced design with good all-round flanking fire provided by circular corner towers and the two gatehouses, one of which is an old fashioned rectangular tower but the other has a pair of D-shaped towers. The lord's chambers were contained in a rectangular tower on one side and opposite it was a large U-shaped tower containing a chapel. This tower was later heightened to make an impressive keep. The keep built on the motte at Sandal probably c1230-50 also had a gateway flanked by twin D-shaped towers. The pair of twin-towered gatehouses built at York in the 1240s and 50s have gone but fragments of the curtain remain with two round towers, and there is a very unusual quatrefoil-shaped keep of two storeys still standing on the motte. This may have been inspired by the keep at Pontefract, a more massive and irregularly planned structure, surrounding rather than surmounting the former motte, probably of six foils, and most likely begun c1210. The best preserved of the early 13th century twin-towered gatehouses in Yorkshire is that at Skipton, although it is partly hidden behind a later porch. The pit of the counterbalanced drawbridge, a feature shared with the other gatehouses of this type, was later vaulted over to make a dungeon. The three other round towers closely grouped around the inner ward are probably of c1220-40.

Middleham Castle

The outer barbican at Sandal

Work of the last third of the 13th century is surprisingly sparse in Yorkshire. Only footings of the gatehouse survive of a new castle built at Sheffield in the 1270s which is thought to have had a circular keep. A thin curtain wall with one small round bastion remains around the keep at Middleham. The gateway at Knaresborough was strengthened c1300 by building solid round towers on either side of it. Only footings remain of a similar project at Pontefract which may never have been completed since later drawings do not show it. One tower remains of a third gateway with solid round towers at Mulgrave. The early 13th century square keep there was given four thinly-walled round corner towers c1300 but very little remains of them. The keep at Sandal has the base of an inner barbican with solid round turrets. Beyond it, probably in the 1290s, was added a D-shaped outer barbican like those at London and Goodrich in Herefordshire. At Sandal the barbican projected into a bailey with a curtain wall and a hall and chambers of about the same date. The mid 13th century inner barbican at Scarborough also had small circular solid turrets. There too there is an outer barbican, a small enclosure of 14th century date with turrets and a twin-towered gateway. The barbicans with twin parallel walls with bartizans on the outer corners added to the four main gateways at York were 14th century work. Only one of them remains. Helmsley has two barbicans, both probably of the mid 13th century. One is little more than a twin-towered gateway with the side walls extended back. The other formed a small outer court with its own corner towers and twin-towered gatehouse.

Edward II (1307-27) erected the King's Tower at Knaresborough during the first half of his reign. It was a splendid lordly residence, rectangular towards the inner ward, but semi-octagonal towards the field. Here the basement, which is vaulted, formed a kitchen or a lodging for an official, and a cellar was provided underneath it, below courtyard level. In the 1320s Edward also built the outer curtain wall at Pickering with three square flanking towers containing lodgings for the use of officials. Both Pickering and Helmsley have early 14th century halls, although both are very ruined. The top stage of the keep at Helmsley also dates from that period.

Scottish raids on the north of England are said to have encouraged the building of tower houses by lesser lords although these buildings were as much status symbols as minor fortresses. Often adjoining a hall (frequently timber-framed), they usually contained a living room for the lord set over a vaulted cellar with a bedroom on the top storey. Tower houses remained in fashion until the early 16th century and many of them cannot be precisely dated. The ruined examples at Ayton and Flamborough are probably two of the earliest. A large and much altered tower surves at Barden. Examples at Aske, Bolton-on-Swale, Bowling, Brough, Cowton, Danby Hall, Hornby and Mortham remain habitable. They vary in size and have all been altered to some degree. Cowton is fairly securely dated to the 1470s. The late 15th century towers at Paull Holme and Riccall are built brick, as is the house with a high turret at Temple Hirst, and there are brick town gateways at both Hull and Beverley.

There are also several fortified manor houses, provided with a moat and thin curtain wall able to offer security against theft and minor raiding. Markenfield, with its complete set of 14th century domestic buildings is the most impressive. Spofforth has a ruined 15th century hall erected over an older basement. Only fragments or foundations remain of other examples at Darfield, Denaby, Haverah Park, Hazlewood, Sherburn and Thornhill. There are also much-altered episcopal residences at Bishopsthorpe and Howden. Farnhill has a hall with four small corner turrets, beyond which project a kitchen at one end a solar at the other. Nappa Hall is an interesting instance of where one of the cross-wings at either end of a domestic hall is carried up to four storeys with battlements. This is evidently more of a status symbol than a fortress since the block is thinly walled and had large windows close to ground level. Many timber-framed manor houses were also moated, partly as a status symbol and partly to give a measure of security against intruders.

Three late 14th century castles, Harewood, Harlsey and Gilling, seem to have been hybrid types, larger and with more rooms on each storey than was normal in a tower house, but not large enough for the rooms to be arranged around a central court. At Harlsey and Gilling only the rectangular basements now remain. Harewood, an important building that deserves to be much better known, was a more complex structure with four corner towers set around a block containing one hall above another, with private chambers in another block at one end. A fourth building of the same period, Whorlton, had a large tower house and a substantial gatehouse, but there is no certain evidence of a curtain wall or other stone buildings.

Middleham Castle

Wressle: window

Hellifield Peel

Lord Scrope's castle at Bolton, begun in the 1370s, seems to have been the first of a new type. It has four lofty ranges of apartments around a fairly small court and four large rectangular corner towers, beside one of which is the entrance. John Neville's castle of the 1380s at Sheriff Hutton was a larger and slightly more irregularly laid out version of this design, whilst Thomas Percy's palace at Wressle had a regular layout with a central gatehouse tower in the middle of one side, but was less defensible since although it had a wet moat the outer walls were quite thin and pierced with large windows. John Neville's son Ralph remodelled the earlier castle at Middleham into a castle of this type with ranges linking corner towers, although the new ranges were quite narrow since the keep still contained the main chambers. Except for Bolton, all these castles originally had an outer court containing offices, stables, workshops and barns. It is likely that the very fragmentary castle of this period at Ravensworth, which had several towers, was divided into inner and outer courts. The Nevilles also built the much more modest castle with ranges around a tiny court at Danby. There the rectangular corner towers project diagonally.

Apart from many tower houses, completely new castles of the 15th century were uncommon in Northern England, and rarely of much military strength. Snape has four small corner towers and is best regarded as an embattled house, probably moated, as was Cawood, where a gatehouse remains. Other 15th century gatehouses remain at Scargill and West Tanfield. At Cawood and West Tanfield the gatehouses have oriel windows facing the field. Crayke has two separate structures of this period. Richard, Duke of Gloucester made improvements to the apartments at Middleham, and during his brief reign as king rebuilt one of the towers at Sandal. At Pontefract the keep was remodelled by John of Gaunt in the late 14th century, and then his son Henry IV (1399-1413) rebuilt several towers of the inner bailey and added a fourth tower as an outlying flanker. The outer ward was walled by one of these two lords, and their immediate successors rebuilt the great hall and provided a new kitchen.

Bolton Castle   *Mulgrave Castle*

In the medieval period castle walls of rubble were sometimes limewashed outside, making them look very different to the way they appear today. Dressed stones around windows and doorways would be left uncovered. Domestic rooms would have had whitewashed rooms decorated with murals of biblical, historical or heroic scenes mostly painted in red, yellow and black. By the 14th century wall hangings decorated with the same themes came into fashion. Although used in churches, glass was expensive and uncommon in secular buildings before the 15th century, so windows were originally closed with wooden shutters. As a result rooms were dark when the weather was too cold or wet for the shutters to be opened for ventilation. The effect of this can be experienced in the recently restored keep at Conisborough. In the later medieval period large openings in the outer walls sometimes had iron bars or grilles protecting them even if high off the ground. Living rooms usually had fireplaces although some halls had central hearths with the smoke escaping through louvres in the roof. Latrines are commonly provided within the thickness of the walls and help to indicate which rooms were intended for living or sleeping in rather than just storage space. At Bolton, Middleham and Sheriff Hutton in the late 14th century latrines were reached from chambers by quite long and winding passageways.

Richmond Castle

Furnishings were sparse up until the 15th century, although the embrasures of upper storey windows often have built-in seats, the earliest examples being in the keep of the 1180s at Conisborough. Lords with several castles tended to circulate around them administering their manorial courts and consuming agricultural produce on the spot. They might also often be away at court or on military or diplomatic service. Their wives or junior family members might be left in residence but often castles were left almost empty, gradually crumbling away with only a skeleton staff in residence to administer the estates. Records of castles needing urgent repairs abound from the 13th century until the period when many of them were abandoned in the 17th century. Garrisons were expensive and after the breakdown of the original system of garrison duty being mandatory for all lesser landowners they were only provided at times of unrest. During periods of conflict even the strongest castles were sometimes captured easily because there was insufficient time or funds available for them to be adequately manned and provisioned against attack. Royal castles were often used by sheriffs and other officials whose personal armed retinue would provide basic security and guard prisoners and stocks of munitions. Servants and clerks often travelled with their lords, and sometimes portable furnishings kept in wooden chests such as rugs, wall-hangings and bedding, and perhaps also cooking utensils, were carried around with their owners. The lord and his immediate family plus honoured guests and the senior household officials would enjoy a fair degree of privacy, having their own rooms. Servants and retainers enjoyed less comfort and privacy, sharing of beds and communal sleeping in the main hall and any other warm places such as the kitchen or stables being common. The early castles had few private rooms but the late 14th century castles once had numerous lodgings.

The hall at Spofforth

Private chambers at Spofforth

The inner ward at Skipton was almost filled with a new set of apartments at the end of the 15th century. The outer gatehouse seems to be also of that period, whilst the long gallery, one of the earliest in England, was added beyond the enceinte just before a wedding in 1536. Otherwise there is not much 16th century work to be seen amongst the major older castles apart from a remodelling of the original hall block at Helmsley to provide more private apartments in the 1580s.

By the time the Civil War broke out in 1642 Sheriff Hutton had already been dismantled and of the major castles Conisborough, Kilton and Pickering were all probably too ruinous to be defensible. Many of the other castles held Royalist garrisons until captured after quite long sieges during 1644-5. After their fall most of them were made untenable. Bolton, Helmsley, Knaresborough, Middleham, Mulgrave, Pontefract, Sandal, Scarborough, Sheffield, Tickhill and Wressle all show signs of dismantling or severe siege damage during this period. Scarborough actually remained in use until the 19th century, since it had artillery batteries commanding the harbour. The castle at York also survived the Civil War, since its court house and prison were still required, although gradual redevelopment of the bailey has swept away all its buildings and most of its curtain wall. Skipton was repaired and re-occupied before the Restoration although later owners transferred themselves outside the claustrophobic inner ward buildings, which are open to the public in a roofed but empty condition. Barden Tower was also patched up after the Civil War but soon allowed to become ruinous. A new barracks was built at Richmond in the 19th century and the keep then repaired. This castle, plus those at Bowes, Conisborough, Helmsley, Middleham, Pickering, Scarborough, and Clifford's Tower at York are all ruins now maintained and opened to the public by English Heritage. The remains at Knaresborough, Pontefract and Sandal are similarly maintained by local authorities.

York: Monk Gate

York: The Multangular Tower

Fireplace in the keep at Scarborough

Fishergate Postern Tower, York

PUBLIC ACCESS TO THE SITES   Codes used in the gazetteers.

E Buildings in the care of English Heritage. Fee payable at some sites.
F Ruins or earthworks to which there is free access at any time.
O Buildings opened to the public by private owners, local councils, trusts.
V Buildings closely visible from public roads, paths, churchyards & open spaces.

FURTHER READING

Castellarium Anglicanum, David Cathcart King, 1983
Castles from the Air, R. Allen Brown, 1989
Castles of Durham & Cleveland, M.J.Jackson, 1996
Castles of North Yorkshire, M.J.Jackson, 2001
Greater Medieval Houses of England & Wales, Vol I, Northern England, A.Emery, 1966
Medieval Buildings of Yorkshire, Peter Ryder, 1982
Moated Sites of Yorkshire, H.E.Jean le Patourel, 1973
Norman Castles in Britain, Derek Renn, 1968
Victoria County Histories of Yorkshire, East Riding, North Riding, various vols.
Yorkshire's Ruined Castles, J.L.Illingworth, 1938
Buildings of England volumes for East Riding (1972), North Riding (1966), and West
    Riding (1959), N.Pevsner
Royal Commission on Historical Monuments: City of York II; The Defences, 1972
See also periodicals such as Country Life, Chateau Gaillard, Archeological Journal,
    Yorkshire Archeological Journal, Transactions of Scarborough Archeological &
    Historical Society, Medieval Archeology.
Guide pamphlets or histories are available for Bolton, Bowes, Conisborough, Danby,
    Helmsley, Knaresborough, Middleham, Pickering, Pontefract, Richmond, Ripley,
    Scarborough, Skipton, Snape, Spofforth, York: Clifford's Tower

GAZETTEER OF YORKSHIRE CASTLES

ACKLAM CASTLE   SE 782613

There are traces here of an eroded or unfinished motte and bailey.

ALDBOROUGH CASTLE   SE 407659

The mutilated earthwork called Studforth Hill just beyond the SE corner of the rampart of the Roman fort of Surium surrounding Aldborough village is probably the site of the castle mentioned in 1115 and 1215 and 1217.

ALMONDBURY: CASTLE HILL   SE 153141

This is a fine defensive site, elevated at 250m and commanding wide views. It consists of a motte at the SW end rising 8m to a summit 50m across, then to the NE is a quadrangular bailey platform about 100m by 90m and beyond that extends an outer enclosure 110m long, possibly used for the original village. When the Jubilee Tower was erected on the motte a well was discovered which was evidently coeval with the earthworks. The castle defended a pass through the Pennines used by the Roman road from Manchester to York and is thought to have been erected in the 1140s as a defence against the Scots, who then held Lancashire north of the Ribble and were laying claim to the whole of that county. It appears that the site was later refortified in stone since a wall was discovered during building work. The site was deserted by Edward II's reign when an inquest was made on the body of a man deposited in the prison of the empty castle after probably being murdered elsewhere.

ARMLEY CASTLE   SE 281338

The earthworks of this motte and bailey castle were removed in 1776 so the grid reference quoted is only approximate.

ASKE HALL   NZ 178034

Behind the east wing is a rather altered 15th century tower. It has an 18th century counterpart behind the west wing. There is a chapel of the 1840s, whilst the south front dates from a remodelling c1960.

Plan of Almondbury Castle

Barden Tower

AUGHTON: CASTLE HILL   SE 702387

The parish church lies in a re-entrant SW angle between a low motte within a square moated platform and a separate bailey platform about 75m square with a ditch 12m wide and 2m deep. Further east is a later moated platform.

Ayton: plan

Ayton Tower

AYTON TOWER   SE 988851   V

This tower is thought to have been built in the 1390s by Ralph Eure, who had obtained the manor by marriage from the de Ayton family. It was sold to James Mauleverer in 1640 and after passing to Edward Stockdale was partly dismantled in the 1670s to provide materials to rebuild the nearby bridge over the River Derwent. The tower measures 16.4m by 10.1m over walls 1.8m thick above a plinth and contained a hall over two vaulted cellars and bedrooms above, although the building is very fragmentary above the vaults, which are carried on transverse ribs. The entrance in the west wall leads through to the northern cellar, which is smaller than its twin since its west wall is thickened to take a spiral stair rather oddly located slightly further south than the NW corner. This arrangement suggests a small room, perhaps a kitchen, was divided off at the north end of the hall, the stair being positioned to give direct access to both parts. The northern cellar had loops facing north and east. The southern cellar has better preserved loops facing east and west and a narrow service stair rises up around the SE corner. The hall has remains of a fireplace on the east and large window embrasures facing south and west.

Ayton: plan

Barden Tower

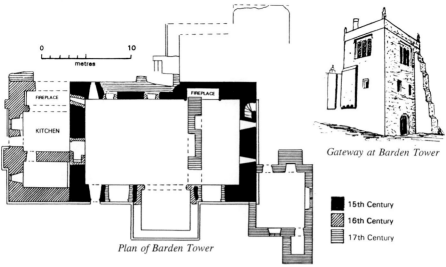

Gateway at Barden Tower

15th Century
16th Century
17th Century

Plan of Barden Tower

BARDEN TOWER   SE 051572   F

Henry, 10th Lord Clifford, who died in 1524, seems to have preferred his hunting seat at Barden to his main seat at Skipton nearby. He is thought to have remodelled the large tower house, which measures 20.3m by 12.7m over walls 1.8m thick, and probably added the block at the west end containing a kitchen and vaulted cellar with two storeys of private rooms above. The projecting bay on the south side is probably later 16th century. The square block adjoining the SE corner and the crosswall partly blocking a large fireplace in the north wall were provided by the Lady Anne Clifford in 1658-9, whose honours and life history are recorded on an inscription over the entrance doorway in the SW corner of the main block. This doorway has a drawbar slot and opened into the service end of a hall, below which were low cellars, probably reached by timber stairs, and now partly filled with earth and rubble. The stairs to the two storeys of upper rooms lay on the north side, where there are two small blocked doorways and the base of another wing either of the late 16th century or the 1650s. This wing had a doorway on the west side. The surrounding courtyard wall was probably dismantled during the Civil War but a simple gateway arch remains at a lower level on the north, whilst to the south is a chapel with mullioned windows adjoining a 16th century tower containing two upper rooms over another gateway. Barden Tower was captured by the rebels during the Pilgrimage of Grace in 1536.

The motte at Barwick-in-Elmet

Barden Tower

BARDSEY: CASTLE HILL   SE 366433   V

An oval mound 3.5m high, 100m long and 30m wide is divided into two enclosures by short sections of ditch with a causeway in between. This site may have been fortified by Adam de Brus after he was granted the manors of Bardsey and Collingham by Henry II.

BARWICK-IN-ELMET CASTLE   SE 398375   F

In the middle of a bailey platform 140m by 95m with a ditch and rampart remaining on the south side, lies a motte rising 10m from the surrounding ditch to an oval summit 26m by 22m. The north end of this summit is at a lower level. Extending for 250m to the north is a village enclosure defended by a rampart and ditch on the east, whilst on the NW the scarps of the defences are more disturbed. Barwick belonged to Ilbert de Lacy at the time of Domesday and the castle was probably built soon afterwards. Henry de Lacy is known to have had a castle here in Stephen's reign.

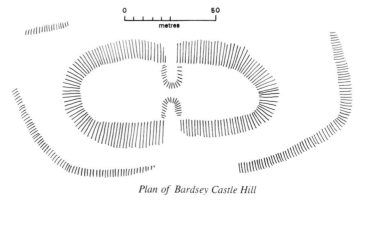

Plan of Bardsey Castle Hill

BAYNARD CASTLE   TA 041331

This is a strongly moated site at Cottingham. A building known as the White House lies on the east side of an outer court 240m long from north to south by 160m wide. A track leads across this court to the Manor House, which lies within a 90m square ditched platform occupying the northern half of the outer court. King John licensed William de Stuteville to fortify his house at Cottingham in 1201, and in 1327 Thomas Wake was licensed to crenellate his house here.

BEDALE CASTLE   SE 265884

The castle said to have been built by Brian Fitz-Alan c1300 lay SW of the church, the tower of which was fortified against the Scots in 1340. Foundations of the castle seem to have still been visible in the mid 19th century. A road lies across the site.

BERGH CASTLE   SE 628670

Cornborough House lies within the outermost of two moated platforms, the overgrown inner one measuring 60m by 30m. This is probably the site of the manor house which Robert de Thweng was licensed to crenellate by Henry III in 1262. It passed by marriage in 1441 to Thomas Witham, Chancellor of the Exchequer to Henry VI and Edward IV, and was probably abandoned after his widow died in 1495.

BEVERLEY TOWN DEFENCES   TA 035394   V

Beverley never had a castle, although the construction of one was mooted in 1149, but the town once had a rampart and ditch with several gatehouses. The surviving gateway known as the North Bar dates from 1409. To build it required 125,000 locally produced bricks of the thin type then in fashion. The passage is vaulted in two bays with brick ribs and has a portcullis groove. There are crow-stepped battlements and blind windows with ogival heads.

BEWERLEY CASTLE   SE 166647

This motte was destroyed c1860.

The tower at Bolling Hall

Town Gateway (North Bar) at Beverley

BISHOPTHORPE PALACE   SE 597478

Part of the moat on the south side remains, together with a fine chapel with lancet windows built by Archbishop Grey in the 1240s. The River Ouse protected the east side, where further 13th century work with lancet windows survives in the basement. The north range has brickwork of the time of Archbishop Thomas Rotherham (1480-1500). Archbishop Frewin rebuilt the east range in the 1660s and Archbishop Drummond added the entrance facade in the Gothick style of the 1760s.

BILTON MOTTE   TA 157326

Swan Hill is a small motte with a water-filled ditch.

BINGLEY TOWER   SE 102398

Nothing remains of this tower and its location is uncertain. The grid reference is that of The Hills where there seems to have once been a motte and bailey,.

Beverley:
plan of North Bar

BOLLING HALL   SE 173314   O

This house (now a museum) just east of Bradford has a medieval tower measuring 7.6m by 6.4m at the south end. It has a turret clasping its SE corner. Much of the rest, including a second tower balancing the other one, dates from the 1660s, but there is a medieval window reset in the north end wall of the west wing. Part of an early 15th century house discovered nearby in 1928 may have been a guest house.

BOLSTERSTONE CASTLE   SK 272968   V

Across the road from the church are remains of a gatehouse, including the small shouldered-lintelled doorway of a room for a guard or porter. The house itself contains 16th ccentury windows but may have older masonry.

Bolton Castle

Bolton Castle

BOLTON CASTLE   SE 034918   O

In September 1378 Sir Richard Scope, Steward of the Household under Richard II, agreed a contract with the mason John Lewyn for the construction of the southern range of this great castle. The wording of the contract suggests that the western and northern ranges had already been built, or at least begun. In July 1379 Sir Richard obtained a licence to crenellate from the boy king to sanction the work already done. Sir Richard later became Chancellor and died in 1403 aged seventy-six. His son Richard had been created Earl of Wiltshire but was executed at Bristol in 1399. According to Leland the castle had been finally completed in that year at a cost of £12,000. In 1537, during the Pilgrimage of Grace, Adam Sedbar, Abbot of Jervaulx, sought safety in the castle. Mary, Queen of Scots was held captive in the castle from July 1568 until she was transferred to Tutbury in Staffordshire in January 1569. John Scope, an illegitimate son of Emmanuel, 11th Lord Scrope, held the castle against a Parliamentary siege from the autumn of 1644 until November 1645. John was subsequently fined £7,000 for his resistance but died aged only twenty before it could be paid. The castle was ordered to be "rendered untenable" by the Parliamentary committee at York in 1647 but it is uncertain how much damage, if any, was then done to it. The collapse of the Kitchen Tower at the NE is recorded in 1761, but the outer walls of this tower, which seems to have borne the brunt of the Parliamentary bombardment, may already have fallen or been dismantled before then. In 1795 the castle passed to Thomas Orde, created Lord Bolton of Bolton Castle two years later. It is still held by his descendants and, famous for its association with Mary, Queen of Scots, it has been a tourist attraction since the early 19th century.

The castle consists of four lofty ranges of apartments set around a court 26m long by 15m wide. The ranges are between 10 and 11m wide except that on the south, which is only 8m wide. The west range has walls 2m thick on each side but in the other ranges the walls towards the court are thinner. Each corner has a five storey tower 10m wide projecting up to 2m beyond the walls. The western towers are 13m long but those at the eastern corners are slightly shorter and that at the NE corner differs from the others in having its long axis from north to south. Each tower has four corner turrets rising slightly higher. The turrets on the corners facing the court project diagonally and are carried on squinch arches with machicolations protecting the doorways below. Two bells were hung on the SW tower, one rung from the courtyard and the other from the adjacent chapel.

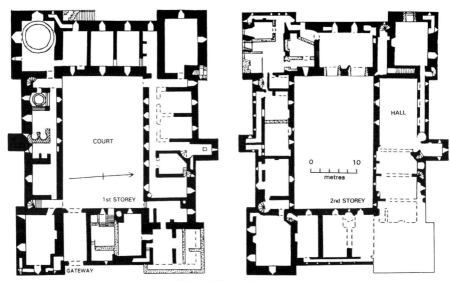

Plans of Bolton Castle

A turret 4.3m wide rises above the middle of the north wall and projects 6m beyond it. In the base of this turret is a prison reached only by a hatch from above. It has an air vent and a latrine. There is a similar but smaller turret containing latrines on the south side, where the castle is loftier because of the slope of the ground. Apart from the damage to the NE corner the castle stands almost complete and the west range and SW tower are still roofed and habitable, having been restored in 1898. This part contains several late 16th century mullioned windows, but these do not detract from the severe appearance of the medieval walls.

Bolton Castle

The entrance passage has a portcullis groove at each end and lies in the east range by the SE tower, which contains a guard room in its basement and a garrison hall above, whilst within its NE corner is a tiny porter's lodge opening off the passage. Off the court led five doorways, all closed by portcullises, one into the east range and one at each end of the north and south ranges. None of them looks more important than another, which would have helped confuse intruders, especially as the windows give little clue as to the disposition of the apartments. The southern doorways lead through to spiral stairs rising to apartments over a bakehouse and brewhouse at courtyard level, with access also to a horse mill in the basement of the SW tower. The third storey of the south range contains the chapel of Anne, with lofty two-light windows towards the court and three cells for chantry priests within the mid-wall turret. East of the chapel is the auditors's chamber, with access to a secret strongroom. The NW doorway was actually the most important of the five. From it there was access to stables in the basement of the west range and a passage led off to several other cellars in the north range and also access to a stair up to a lobby in the north mid-wall turret, from which there was access to the two storey hall located in the western half of that range. The east half of the range, now much ruined, contained rooms for storing and preparing food and there was access at two levels to a well. The hall had a central hearth with the smoke escaping up flues in the window heads. Over the service passage at the east end lay a musicians' gallery. A passage in the hall north wall led to a private chamber with a latrine, fireplace and two windows in the NW tower. A spiral stair leads up to similar chambers above. Immediately south of this tower was a passage leading from the hall SW corner to a fine chamber in the west range. A spiral stair at the end of the passage leads up to an even grander chamber on the third storey above. This occupies the whole of the range except for the room once claimed to be Queen Mary's bedroom at the south end. A passage leads past the bedchamber to the third storey room in the SW tower, which has access to the spiral stair in the south range SW corner, beyond which is a doorway to the chapel.

BOLTON-ON-SWALE HALL   SE 253991

This building, remodelled in the 18th century, comprised a hall block lying between a three storey solar tower and a second cross-wing which has been removed.

Bowes Castle

BOWES CASTLE   NY 992134   F

It was probably Alan, Count of Brittany and Earl of Richmond from 1137 onwards, who created a ditched platform in the NW corner of the former Roman fort of Lavatrae. The remainder of the fort formed an outer bailey and contains the parish church in its NE corner. It would appear that the stone keep was begun by Alan's son Conan and was completed after his death in 1171 by Henry II, who married Conan's daughter Constance to his son Geoffrey. Their children suffered at the hands of King John (who visited Bowes twice), Arthur being murdered, and Eleanor being kept at Bowes before being taken down south to Corfe. In the mid 13th century Bowes was held by Peter de Savoy. In 1322 Edward II granted Bowes to John de Scargill but it was besieged and captured by local lords hostile to John. The castle seems to have suffered considerable damage, being described in 1342 as "ruinous, untenable and of no value". It reverted to the Crown in 1361 and was later granted to the Nevilles. After Richard Neville's defeat and death in 1471 Bowes again reverted to the Crown. James I sold the castle to the City of London. The keep may have remained habitable until the Civil War, its demolition being attributed to General Lambert.

The keep now stands 15m high and measures 24.4m by 17.8m over walls 3.6m thick above a battered plinth from which rise broad pilaster buttresses at the corners and in the middle of each side. It contained two rooms on each of two storeys, although very little remains of the crosswall. The lower rooms were dimly lighted by narrow loops are were reached from above by a wide spiral stair in the SE corner. The upper storey contained a hall on the east and a private room on the west, both having latrines in the SW corner, that from the hall needing a long passage to reach it. Neither room retains a fireplace, so there must have been central hearths. The private room had one large window and one narrow loop facing west. The hall had a large window in each of the south and north walls, whilst the east wall contained the entrance, flanked on either side by mural rooms, and reached by a long flight of steps outside up to some sort of porch or forebuilding. There is no evidence that the bailey ever possessed a stone curtain wall or other stone buildings.

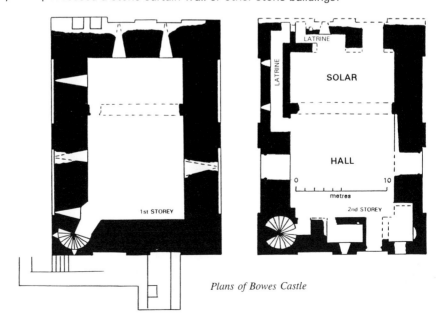

Plans of Bowes Castle

Castle Hill, Burton-in-Lonsdale

BRADFIELD: BAILEY HILL   SK 266927

The ditched motte of the Bailey Hill rises as high as 18m but only part remains of the summit, which is said to have once been 12m across. The bailey platform to the west was defended by a steep natural drop on the west and has a 9m high rampart on the south side. There seems to have been a later stone castle including a keep upon Castle Hill at SK 271923 but only shapeless earthworks remain there now.

BRIDLINGTON PRIORY   TA 177680

The priory was fortified or provided with a strongpoint in 1143 but this was seized by William le Gros, Count of Aumale.

BROMPTON MOTTE   SE 945821   V

On the summit of the Castle Hill measuring 55m by 30m across are traces of buildings. There is thought to have once been a motte on the north side. The castle was either founded by Berenger de Todeni in the 11th century or by Eustace Fitz-John, who was granted the manor by Henry I.

BROUGH HALL   SE 220978

A medieval tower house was remodelled c1560 into an Elizabethan house of three storeys and three bays. This in turn was altered and given a new facade c1730, but older masonry survives at the back. The wings on each side are of 1790.

BURTON-IN-LONSDALE: CASTLE HILL   SD 649722   V

Excavations revealed footings of a stone wall around the 40m long by 20m wide summit of the 10m high oval motte. The motte top was found by the excavators to be paved with stones bedded in clay. Similar pavings were found on the rampart slopes and in the ditch bottom. A bailey platform 30m by 20m lies to the south, and a larger but less well-defended second bailey 60m by 50m lies to the west. This castle is generally assumed to have been erected by Robert de Mowbray, who was disinherited by William Rufus after his rebellion in 1095.

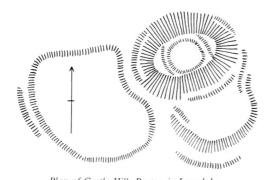

Plan of Castle Hill, Burton-in-Lonsdale

BUTTERCRAMBE CASTLE SE 733586

In the grounds of Aldby Park is a motte rising 8m above its ditch to a summit 12m across and a small bailey platform which is eroded on the NE, which overlooks a drop towards the River Derwent. Robert de Stuteville, the probable builder, was forfeited in 1106 for rebelling against Henry I. King Stephen restored the manor to his grandson Robert, and in 1201 his son William de Stuteville obtained a licence to crenellate his house here. There is said to have been a "well built" capital messuage here in 1282, but this may have stood on the site of the present mansion of Aldby, which itself replaced a house destroyed by fire in the mid 17th century. The manor passed in 1232 to the Wakes and then in 1349 went by marriage to the Hollands, later Earls of Kent. It may have then been abandoned.

CARLTON CASTLE SE 068846

Beside a stream behind the Forester's Arms is a mound rising 4m above a ditch 2m deep to a summit 9m across. It was perhaps an outpost of Middleham.

CASTLE HOWARD SE 716700 O

Plan of Bailey Hill, Bradfield

```
0                    50
|  |  |  |  |  |  |
       metres
```

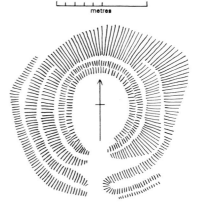

Plan of Castle Levington

The huge Baroque mansion begun in 1700 for the 3rd Earl of Carlisle stands on or very near the site of the late medieval castle of Henderskelf, described by Leland as a quadrangular building with four towers. A house belonging to the Greystokes, originally unfortified, stood on the site in 1359. The towers were probably added c1500 by Thomas, Lord Dacre, who obtained it by marriage. In 1571 the property passed by marriage to Philip Howard, a son of the 4th Duke of Norfolk. Henderskelf Castle was rebuilt in 1684 by Edward Howard, but was destroyed by a fire in 1693.

CASTLE LEVINGTON   NZ 461103

On a bluff rising 35m above the River Leven is a ringwork measuring about 60m by 55m. The rampart rises 2m above the interior and 9m above the ditch isolating the site on the SW side. On the SE side is a platform 60m long by just 6m wide. This was an early seat of the de Brus family, the manor having been given by Henry I to Robert de Brus. Since Adam de Brus was a strong supporter of King Stephen it is likely that Henry II had the castle dismantled in the late 1150s. A timber hall was built on the site by Nicholas de Meynel after he acquired the manor in 1272. See p 27.

CASTLETON: CASTLE HILL   NZ 688082   V

Castle House in the village of Castleton lies within a ringwork about 55m by 35m across with a rampart up to 6m high. In the 19th century a tower was said to remain on the south side and part of a curtain wall on the north, and there are reports of Norman window mullions being found on the site, but excavations in 1988 revealed no signs of masonry. This site is thought to have been fortified by Robert de Brus in the 1090s as the centre of his estates in Cleveland, only to be superseded by the larger castle at Skelton. It was acquired by William le Gros, Count of Aumale in the late 1150s, and was held by the Crown from his death in 1179 until sold to Peter de Brus c1200. This site is assumed to be the castle of "Daneby" recorded in 1242. It was occupied by Marmaduke de Thweng in 1275 in preference to his other seat at Kilton. It passed in 1294 to William de Latimer, who entertained Edward II at his castle here in 1323. Since it was described in 1335 as "a ruined peel" and saw no further use, the site is assumed to have been destroyed during a Scottish raid.

CATTERICK MOTTE   SE 240981

The churchyard may be the former bailey measuring 95m by 70m of an adjoining motte known as Palet Hill which rises up to 5m to a summit 11m across.

Castle Hill, Castleton

Cawaood Castle

Cawood Castle

CAWOOD CASTLE   SE 575376   V

Cawood is mentioned in 1181 as a residence of the Archbishops of York and the innermost of the two moats may be of that period. Archbishop Neville, d1391 is said to have rebuilt the castle but the main surviving part, a gatehouse of white stone, dates from the time of Archbishop Kempe, d1451. It has a four-centred arch and a passageway with a tierceron vault, there being dual inner arches for carriages and pedestrians. The second storey has oriel windows both to the field and to the former court and there is a third storey above, whilst a stair turret rises even higher. To the east and west of the gatehouse are brick ranges, that to the east having cusped single light windows in oblong frames between buttresses.

CLIFTON CASTLE   SE 218842

The existing building of 1802-10 erected by John Hutton is said to incorporate a length of wall from the manor house which Geoffrey de Scope was licensed to crenellate by Edward II in 1317, and which Leland described as "like a pele or castelet". An old drawing shows a ruined wall with a large arch and a stepped buttress. The castle passed from the Scropes to Sir Christopher Danby and then went to Sir Marmaduke Wyville. The Daltons family sold it to the Huttons c1735.

CONISBOROUGH CASTLE   SK 514989   E

Although this castle is not mentioned until the 1170s, it is assumed to have been founded a hundred years earlier by William de Warenne, a companion of William I, who was created Earl of Surrey just before his death in June 1088 by William II. His grandson, William, 3rd Earl, died on crusade in 1147, leaving a daughter, Isabel. Her first and second husbands, William of Blois, d1159, and Hamelin Plantagenet, an illegitimate half-brother of Henry II in turn became the fourth and fifth earls. Hamelin held Conisborough from 1163 until his death in 1202 and around 1180 he began rebuilding it as a strong stone castle with a circular keep and curtain wall. He had recently also built another circular keep at his castle at Mortemer in Normandy. John, the eighth earl, Hamelin's great-great grandson, succeeded his father John as a minor in 1304. He invoked the wrath of Thomas, Earl of Lancaster by abducting the latter's wife Alice. Conisborough was captured by Earl Thomas and held by him until his defeat and execution by Edward II in March 1322. It was returned to Earl John in 1326, but reverted to the Crown on his death without an heir in 1347.

Edward III gave Conisborough to his youngest son Edmund of Langley, but since he was a child the estate was administered by his mother, Queen Philippa. The domestic buildings seem to have been remodelled at this time. Edmund was made Earl of Cambridge and his nephew Richard II later made him Duke of York. His sons both died in 1415, Edward, Duke of Albermarle being killed at Agincourt, whilst Richard, Earl of Cambridge was executed for treason. Richard's widow held the castle in dower until her death in 1446 and made it her residence. The then neglected castle became a Crown possession when Edward IV took the throne in 1461, although repairs were executed in 1482-3. Henry VIII granted the castle to the Carey family. By 1538 it was in a poor state, the gates and bridge having collapsed, along with the top floor of the keep and most of the curtain wall on the south side. The castle thus saw no further use and the keep was saved from being slighted during the Civil War.

Conisborough Castle

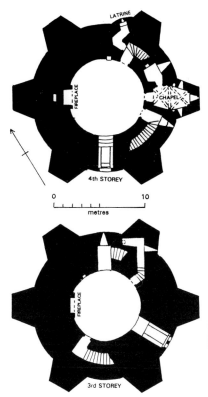

Conisborough: plans of keep

Keep at Conisborough

The castle has a single D-shaped court 70m long by 45m wide but originally there was an outer court defended by a palisade and ditch to the west. The inner court is surrounded by a 10m high curtain wall between 2.2m and 2.7m thick still complete to the wall-walk except for short lengths on the west and north which were refaced externally in the 14th century and a 35m long section on the south side which was destroyed by a landslip probably in the early 16th century. The wall was flanked and commanded by eight semi-circular turrets, of varying sizes up to 4m in diameter, five of which have been destroyed, including the two that flanked the entrance, which were later refaced in ashlar, with a new archway between them. The north side has three pilaster buttresses but no turrets. There are no posterns and the only entrance was through an inwardly projecting gatehouse on the south side, most of which has fallen. This gateway was closed by a portcullis and was approached by a 13th century barbican in the form of a zig-zag passageway just over 3m wide. There is a latrine in the curtain wall on the east side of the keep. Abutted against all sides of the curtain were rooms. West of the gateway was a guard room over a pit prison with a latrine. East of the gateway lay the chapel. On the north side was a hall with a central hearth and a central row of pillars. A kitchen and other service rooms lay between it and the keep. Private rooms lay on the west side, where there is a latrine built over a fissure in the rock. In the later remodelling an extra pair of rooms were created by cutting off the west end of the hall.

The keep slightly predates the curtain, which abuts against it. The relationship between the two, with just a short section of the keep projecting out of a re-entrant angle of the bailey wall (allowing latrines high up on the keep to discharge outside the bailey) recalls the layout of the keep and inner ward of Richard I's mighty castle of Chateau Gaillard in Normandy built in 1197-8, just after Conisborough. The keep is one of the finest and strongest medieval secular structures in Britain. Faced inside and out with the finest quality limestone ashlar, and strengthened by six huge evenly spaced buttresses without parallel anywhere else in Britain, it measures 15m in diameter over walls 4.5m thick above a tall battered plinth with steps on the sides of the buttresses. In 1994 the ruin was provided with new floors and a conical roof within the wall-walk 23m above the court. A new stair rises up over the remains of a stair to a doorway with a joggled lintel. This leads into a circular room without windows. Below is a vaulted basement reached only by a hatch in the crown of its vault, allowing water to be drawn from a well without having to descend to the basement. Stairs within the curve of the wall lead to a private room with a fireplace on the NW, a latrine on the NE and a single south-facing window of two rectangular lights set in a deep embrasure fitted with seats. One has to cross this room to reach another stair to the topmost room, with a similar layout, except that a small chapel of elongated hexagonal plan is squeezed into the eastern buttress. The doorways here are set in sections of straight walling as if the room was intended to be octagonal. Upper vaults were possibly intended but the keep would have had to have been 5m higher to fit them in. The chapel has a round-headed east window with a roll-moulding set under an arch with chevrons, whilst on either side are quatrefoil shaped loops. Vaulted in two bays with a rib flanked by chevrons, the chapel has a piscina and a doorway on the north leads into a sacristy. Again one has to traverse the main room to reach the stair to the wall-walk, off which there is access to a dovecote, an oven and two cisterns within the buttresses, which rose one stage higher as turrets.

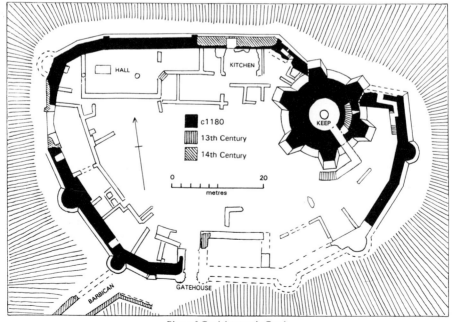

Plan of Conisborough Castle

CONSTABLE BURTON CASTLE   SE 163911

The hall built in 1762-8 by Sir Marmaduke Asty Wyvill stands on the site of a house which Geoffrey le Scrope was licensed to crenellate by Edward III in 1338. He had acquired the manor from the de Richmond family in 1321. It passed in 1517 to Sir Ralph Fitz-Randall and then c1550 to Sir Marmaduke Wyville. He remodelled the house and entertained Queen Elizabeth there.

COTHERSTONE CASTLE   NZ 013200

The masonry remains on the motte may date from 1201, when King John licenced fortifications here.

Collapsed gateway turret at Conisborough

COWTON CASTLE   NZ 294023

A panel over the entrance tells us this tower house was erected by Sir Richard Conyers. In c1472 he obtained the manor, formerly held by the Nevilles, from Richard, Duke of Gloucester and the castle was described in 1487 as newly built. It passed to the Bowes family c1538, and then from 1605 had a succession of owners, who let it to tenants, as is still the case. The tower measures 18m by 7.5m externally and until altered in the mid 18th century contained two lofty chambers one above the other at the south end, whilst the northern part contained four storeys of rooms linked by a spiral staircase in a turret on the east side and served by latrines in a turret on the west side. Both turrets are square and rise one stage above the battlements of the main building. The entrance lay at the foot of the staircase. The tower was originally surrounded by a low outer wall, but the last remains of its gateway on the west side were destroyed in the 1950s. The main building lost part of its roof in 1979 but has since been restored.

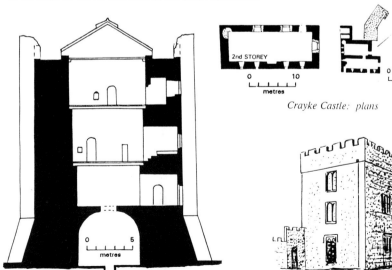

Crayke Castle: plans

Conisborough: section of keep

Cowton Castle

Danby Castle

CRAYKE CASTLE   SE 559707

The first mention of this motte and bailey castle of the Bishops of Durham is in King John's reign, when it was captured by one of his mercenary captains, Faulkes de Breaute. In 1217 William Marshall, acting as regent for the young Henry III, ordered Faulkes to hand over the castle to the Bishop of Chichester. Anthony Bek, bishop from 1284 to 1311, is said to have rebuilt the castle in stone. In 1345 Edward III stayed within it and issued orders allowing the election of a new bishop. Most of the existing remains appear to be the work of Robert Neville, bishop from 1438 to 1457. Under pressure Bishop Richard Barnes leased the castle to Queen Elizabeth and she in turn leased it to a series of tenants. In 1648 the castle was sold off by Parliamentary trustees and after this time may have been partly dismantled. It was restored to Bishop John Cosin in the 1660s and the chamber block was patched up as a farmhouse. Bishop William Van Mildert sold off the property c1830 and it has changed hands several times since. In 1923 the chamber block was described as having been recently restored and currently in use as a shooting box.

The principal remnant is a block which contained a long narrow great chamber with a fireplace in the middle of the SE in which are four windows. Below was a cellar and above are two upper storeys of bedrooms. The NW facing windows of the great chamber were obscured when a kitchen was formed on that side over rib-vaulted basement. Originally both kitchen and great chamber had spiral staircases in their respective western corners but there has been much 18th and 19th century rebuilding and a range of that period stands on the site of what is thought to have been a timber-framed hall. Only the lowest stage remains of an L-planned building called the New Tower to the south. It stood four storeys high in the 1560s but was then in a perilous condition. It seems to have contained a smaller hall and chamber over vaulted rooms.

CROPTON: T'HALL GARTH   SE 755893   F

A worn down motte 4m high lies towards the west end of a platform about 110m across with a rampart on the north but whatever defences existed on the east have gone. Immediately east of the motte are the buried footings of a manor house thought to have been erected by Baldwin de Wake c1250. His father Hugh inherited the manor on the death of Robert de Stuteville in 1241. The Robert de Stuteville who was forfeited by Henry I in 1106 may have built the motte and bailey earthworks.

CUSWORTH: CASTLE HILL   SE 542033

This motte rises 5m to a summit 18m across from a ditch which was cut through rock on the west, whilst it has been mostly filled in on the east. Cusworth was held by the Warennes as part of the Honour of Conisbrough.

DANBY CASTLE   NZ 717072   V

An estate here was inherited by John de Neville from the Latimers in 1381 and either John, or his son (another John) are assumed to have built the castle, which superseded the ringwork at Castleton. On the death of Ralph Neville, 2nd Earl of Westmorland Danby passed to his third son George, created Lord Latimer by Henry VI in 1432. John Neville, Lord Latimer, died in 1577 leaving several daughters, one of which married Sir John Danvers. Their son Henry became Earl of Danby but by then the castle from which the title was taken was probably leased to tenant farmers. The castle was sold in 1656 to John Dawnay, whose descendants still own it.

The castle has an unusual layout with four towers projecting diagonally from the corners of what is essentially a square of about 25m, except that the kitchen range projects outside the square, thus filling most of the space between the two northern towers, which are 8m wide. Little remains of the SW tower, whilst the 6m wide SE tower now forms part of the present farmhouse with a modern extension beyond it. This tower was given an extra third storey with a hammer-beam roof when rebuilt in the late 16th century with a projecting chimney stack on one side. Parts of the castle outer walls were only about 1m thick and are missing on the east side (demolished in 1745) and on the west, whilst the walls of the north towers are thicker but contain vulnerable latrines with thin outer walling. The 12m long by 6m wide kitchen has two large fireplaces and a smoke room in the SW corner. The shields on the outer wall here with the arms of the Roos and Latimer families may be older work reset. The hall on the east side was 18m long by 9m wide, leaving only a 7m wide court between it and the mostly destroyed west range, in which was the gateway. The hall inner wall contains doorways at either end of a set of four windows of two lights. In the south range is a rib-vaulted cellar under what was the lord's private room, divided into a court room and jury room in the 16th century, new windows then being inserted. This part was restored after a chimney stack collapsed in 1960.

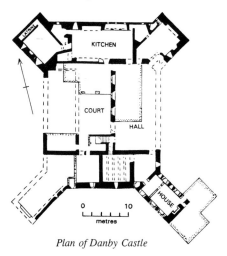

Plan of Danby Castle

Crayke Castle

Danby Castle: SE Tower

DANBY HALL   SE 159871

This building has a 14th or 15th century embattled tower as its core. The east side of the mansion is 16th century but was remodelled in 1658 with mullion-and-transom windows, whilst the south front is of 1855 and the porch is of 1904.

DARFIELD: NEW HALL   SE 394052

The present house mostly of 19th and 20th century date lies in the NE corner of a court about 55m long by about 30m at the widest end towards the east. The former wet moat has been mostly filled in but the fairly thin outer wall on the NW and west is medieval, with traces of adjacent ranges, and medieval footings survive under the modern wall on the south. From the early 13th century until the 1630s New Hall was held by the Bosvile family, later passing to the Wortleys and then the Mardens.

DENABY OLD HALL   SK 483991

One range of this late medieval courtyard house had gone by the 1830s and now only half of one range survives made into a cottage. It retains a latrine turret, a staircase projection, and one or two medieval windows.

DONCASTER CASTLE

Nothing remains of the castle at Doncaster mentioned by Leland nor does anything survive of the town gateways he mentions, or the rampart which is assumed to have been raised in 1193 when the town was fortified against the rebellious Prince John.

DRAX CASTLE   SE 676260

The castle here which King Stephen had destroyed in 1154 may have been where there is now a large moated platform.

Farnhill Hall

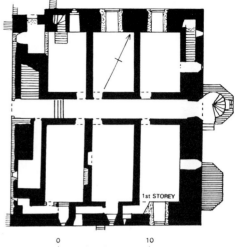

1st STOREY

0   10
metres

Plan of Gilling Castle

DRIFFIELD CASTLE   TA 023583

There are slight remains of a motte and bailey castle mentioned during the reigns of Stephen and John.

EASBY CASTLE   NZ 589084

A ringwork 30m across, damaged on the SE side, where it overlooks a slope, lies near High Farm. It was probably built in the 1140s by Bernard de Balliol.

ELSLACK TOWER

Edward II issued a licence to embattle a tower at "Estlake in Craven" in 1318.

FARNHILL HALL   SE 003465

This building consisted of a main block 30m long by 10m wide over walls 1.3m thick containing a hall with a kitchen at the west end and a solar at the west end. Set not at the corners of the whole block but at the corners of the central hall are small square embattled turrets. That on the NE contains a stair up to the roof and the others contain tiny rooms. One might expect these to be latrines but no outlets are visible. The hall was probably built by Robert Fernhill shortly after an older house had been destroyed by the Scots during their incursion of 1314. Farnhill was later sold to the Copley family and then passed in the early 15th century to the Eltofts, who held it until 1636. They created an extra room over the solar in the late 16th century. Most of the original windows are now blocked or were replaced in the 1830s.

FELIXKIRK CASTLE   SE 468846

On a spur at the south end of the village is a motte called Howe Hill rising 4m to a summit 6m across, probably built in the 1140s by Robert Fossard. The site must have been abandoned by 1210, when it was sold to the church.

FENWICK CASTLE   SE 582150

Only a manorial moat lies on the assumed site of the castle mentioned in 1272.

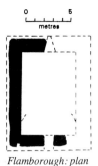

Flamborough: plan

Gilling Castle

FLAMBOROUGH TOWER   TA 226703

North of the church are earthworks and three defaced walls of a tower probably built around the time of the licence to crenellate obtained by Marmaduke Constable from Edward III in 1351. The ruins include one west facing loop and an east doorway. William the Constable had obtained a licence for an oratory here in 1315. A tower, hall, great parlour, lord's parlour, chapel, court-house, mill-house and great barn are mentioned in 1537 upon the death of Sir Robert Constable, but around that time Leland described the place as "taken rather for a manor place than a castle". The vaulted cellar in the tower was being used for cattle in 1798. The vault was described in 1885 as having eight stone ribs with chalk blocks between them. There is also mention of the staircase being reached through a doorway with an ogival head.

GILLING CASTLE   SE 612769

Only the basement now survives of a building constructed by Thomas de Etton, who died c1395. It measures 24m by 21m over walls 3m thick, except that the west wall was still thicker. This side contained the entrance with heraldic shields (now hidden behind an external 18th century staircase) with chambers south of it and a straight stair to the upper parts leading off north from it. The entrance led onto a central passage, passing three vaulted rooms on each side, and then running though to a back doorway now contained within one of a pair of 16th century polygonal bays on the east side. The three northern rooms lay under the hall and formed cellars, two of them having service stairs leading up. All three southern rooms have latrines and two have fireplaces so they must have been offices or private rooms, although since the rooms with fireplaces were each lighted only by a single narrow loop in the south wall they would have been very dark. The other room has an east facing loop in addition and now has above it the fine great chamber of c1580 with a huge chimney-piece, a painted family tree frieze with over 370 coats of arms and large mullion-and-transom windows. This Elizabethan rebuilding of the upper storeys was the work of Sir William Fairfax, his family being in possession of Gilling from 1492 to 1793. The castle had been forfeited by Humphrey Neville in 1461 and was then held until 1485 by Sir Edmund Hastings. The lower ranges to the NW and SW, leaving an open court west of the older main block, look early 18th century, although the south wing is at least partly late 16th century with a chimney-piece and two mullioned windows of that date. The castle was sold and converted into a school in the early 20th century.

Gilling Castle

Flamborough Tower

GISBURN: CASTLE HAUGH SD 830508

Part of this earthwork, which was the seat of the Percy estates in the district of Craven, has collapsed down into the River Ribble below. The remainder is a 6m high motte with a dished summit 27m across and a surrounding ditch 2m deep.

GRINTON CASTLE SE 049984

Between the cemetery and the River Swale are two enclosures. The eastern one is about 50m square. The western one is triangular and has on the NW side, above a steep natural slope, traces of a wall. The other sides have a ditch 9m wide.

GUISBOROUGH PRIORY NZ 611694

Edward III licensed the prior of Guisborough to crenellate his dwelling at the priory but what, if anything, was constructed under the terms of this licence is unknown. In 1376 the prior and convent were granted a second licence to embattle the walls of the priory precinct.

HAMERTON HALL SD 719538

Lying to the north of Slaidburn, beside the ravine of the River Hodder, this was the original seat of the Hamerton family. The existing building is mostly late 16th or early 17th century but the spiral stair in the NE corner of the west cross-wing may be a relic of an earlier embattled wing or tower house.

HANGTWAITE: CASTLE HILLS SE 551067

A 5m high motte lies SW of a kidney-shaped bailey with a rampart 3m high. On the west the ditch partly contains water and has an outer bank. On the east is a triangular outer platform. The Radcliffe Moat lies only 0.3km to the east.

Harewood Castle

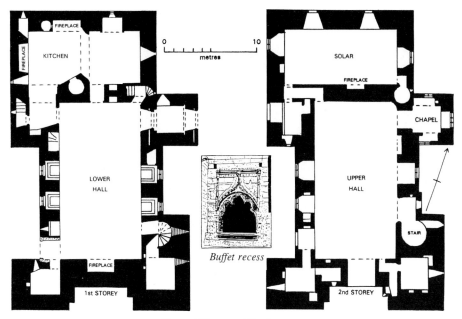

Plans of Harewood Castle

HAREWOOD CASTLE   SE 322456

There is said to have been a castle at Harewood in the 12th century, perhaps where there are slight earthworks at SE 296463, but the existing building was built by Sir William Aldburgh, who was licensed by Edward III to crenellate it in 1367. It was subsequently shared by several generations of the descendants of his daughters Elizabeth and Sybil, who married Sir Richard Redmayne and Sir William Ryther. This arrangement lasted until 1630, with the families living in the castle either alternately or together. Effigies of Elizabeth and Sybil and their husbands remain in the parish church. The Redmaynes later intermarried with the Gascoignes of Gawthorp Hall, the site of which lies under the lake in the park. The castle is a curious structure very oddly built against a slope. The surroundings are too overgrown for any remains of outworks or other buildings to be visible. Walls up to 2.8m thick enclose a fine hall with a pair of centrally placed two-light windows on each of the east and west sides, a buffet recess on the west with a richly cusped arch and a fireplace at the south end. At the corners are towers, all roughly 6m by 5.2m although in fact no two of them are an exact match for size or shape. They all contain five levels of chambers, most of them being bedrooms with fireplaces and latrines. The lowest level of the NE tower formed a porch with a portcullis groove and two draw-bar slots, whilst a room higher up with a three light east window was evidently a chapel. A wide spiral stair in a north extension of the SE tower leads up to a second hall above. Beyond the north end of the two halls is a cross-wing containing a kitchen and pantry at the level of the lower hall, a vaulted cellar and a guard room below, and two large and fine private chambers above. Both these chambers have access to a narrower spiral stair located near the porch. The kitchen has fireplaces on the north and west sides and an oven in the NW corner. It was reached from the lower hall by a servery in the NW tower, where a straight mural stair leads down to the cellar, in which is a well.

Harlsey Castle

HARLSEY CASTLE   SE 415981

The remains of the castle built c1430 by Sir James Strangways, a judge of the Common Pleas, comprise the basement about 5m high of a tower house 25m long by 15m containing three vaulted cellars, plus an enclosure 140m by 115m with three arms remaining of a wet moat 9m wide, now the garden of a farmhouse. Not far from the west side of the site is a steep drop. It passed to the Dacre family in 1541 but was forfeited after Leonard Dacre took part in the rebellion of 1569 and given to Henry Carey, Lord Hunsdon. The Dacres obtained the castle back again in 1663 and it passed to the Howards and then to the Earls of Harewood. The upper parts of the tower house seem to have been dismantled c1820 after being damaged by lightning.

HAVERAH PARK   SE 220545

Strongly sited on the end of a spur at Haverah Park, is a ditched platform about 35m by 30m which seems to have had a curtain wall and gatehouse, with a bridge over the moat. Within are buried footings of a central tower about 15m square and one wall which probably formed part of a range backing onto the curtain. Haverah Park was a hunting seat within the royal lordship of Knaresborough and there are several records of a "fortalicium" in the park. Edward III had building works in progress here in 1334. In 1372 he granted it along with Knaresborough to his son John of Gaunt.

HAZLEWOOD CASTLE   SE 449398

This building was remodelled as a two storey Georgian house in the 1760s, but the entrance hall is in fact the much altered great hall of the castle which Sir William Vavasour was licensed by Edward I to crenellate in 1290. One window with a shouldered lintel has been exposed on the north side and there is a spiral staircase in the NW corner, beyond which is a tower with a 15th century upper window facing north. At the east end of the building is a little altered late 13th century chapel with an original doorway and windows with Y-tracery. Sir William was licensed to build a chapel here in 1286. The chapel contains effigies of several medieval Vavasours, plus those of Sir Thomas, d1632, and Sir Walter, d1713, with their wives.

HELLIFIELD PEEL SD 859556

In 1440 Henry VI licensed Laurence Hamerton (grandson of Adam, the first Hamerton owner of Hellifield) to "enclose, crenellate and furnish with towers and battlements his manor of Helefeld". It would appear that about that time wings about 4.2m wide were added at either end of the west side of a three storey 14th century solar tower 14.8m long by 7.8m wide which was itself an addition to a long-lost aisled hall to the east. The original tower had a spiral stair in a turret projecting from the north end of the east wall and in the 15th century remodelling a small extension was made to this part onto the site of where the former hall had stood. A crosswall, now totally collapsed, was also inserted in the main building. A blocked piscina betrays the former presence of a chapel at the south end of the third storey. The chapel east window was later converted into a mullion-and-transom window of three lights. It appears that the main Hamerton residence in later years was Wigglesworth Hall, lying to the east. Hellifield seems to have been held by wives and widows as a dower house and in 1536 Dame Elizabeth refused admission to Hellifield to her own second husband Edward Stanley, stones being thrown down on his party from the tower. Her son Sir Stephen Hamerton was executed in 1537 for his part (even if under coercion) in the Pilgrimage of Grace. Hellifield was later granted to George Browne and later passed to the Darcys but both these families had connections with the Hamertons, who managed to regain possession of the peel in the 1560s. See page 11.

In the 17th century a wing was added into the space between the two wings or turrets on the west side of the building and a number of new windows were inserted. Further large new sash windows were inserted during the 18th century and work was also carried out in the 19th century. Dorothy Hamerton, last of her line, sold the estate in 1948 and the house was then abandoned and the lead roof removed.

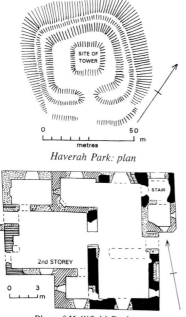

Haverah Park: plan

Plan of Hellifield Peel

Hazlewood Castle

HELMSLEY CASTLE   SE 611836   E

The unusual double circuit of ditches here may have been a symbol of regality, in which case they must go back to the time of Domesday Book in 1087 when Helmsley was held by William I's half brother Robert de Mortain, whose castle of Berkampstead in Hertfordshire was also double ditched. He was forfeited in 1088 by his nephew William II and from at least the 1120s Helmsley was held by the l'Espec family. Walter l'Espec retired in 1154 to the abbey of Rievaulx that he had founded, and his estates passed to his sister Adeline and her husband Peter de Roos. Robert de Roos rebuilt the castle in stone during his long tenure of the lordship from 1186 to 1227. His grandson Robert, lord of Helmsley 1258 to 1285, married Isabel, heiress of Belvoir in Leicestershire. The keep and curtain walls at Helmsley were heightened in the 14th century as a response to Scottish raids, probably by their grandson William, who succeeded as Lord Ros of Helmsley and Belvoir in 1316.

In 1478 Edmund de Roos sold Helmsley to Richard, Duke of Gloucester but it was returned to Edmund by Henry VII after Richard's defeat and death at Bosworth. After Edmund died childless in 1508 Helmsley passed to Sir George Manners of Etal in Northumberland, the son of Edmund's sister Eleanor. He thus became the 12th Lord Ros. His son Thomas was created Earl of Rutland by Henry VIII in 1525. The arms of Edward, 3rd Earl and his wife Isabel Holcroft appear on the plasterwork in the domestic buildings, which were remodelled for them. Edward was succeeded by his brother John and then in turn by each of his nephews, Roger and Francis. On his death in 1632 the latter left a daughter, Katherine, who was married to the son of the first Duke of Buckingham. In November 1644 a Royalist garrison under Sir Jordan Crosland surrendered to Sir Thomas Fairfax after a three month siege. After returning from exile in 1657 the 2nd Duke of Buckingham married Sir Thomas's daughter Mary Fairfax and a previous connection between the families may explain why the domestic buildings remained habitable after the curtain walls were destroyed by order of Parliament. After the Duke died in retirement at Helmsley in 1688, the castle was sold to the London banker Charles Duncombe, who probably began the mansion Duncombe Park which replaced the castle as the family residence shortly before his death in 1711. The husband of his sister and heiress Mary then changed his name to Duncombe. Their descendants became Earls of Feversham and still own the castle, although it has long been in State guardianship.

Outer gatehouse at Helmsley

Portcullis groove
in outer gatehouse

Helmsley Castle   *The keep at Helmsley*

The castle consists of a single quadrangular court 100m long by up to 65m wide surrounded by a deep and steeply sided ditch enclosed by an outer rampart with its own ditch. The site is quite rocky, there being outcrops on both sides of the ditch on the SW side and in the inner sides of both ditches at the SE end. The 2m thick curtain wall has been mostly been reduced to less than 2m high. The wall-walk was about 4m above the court until the walls were heightened in the 14th century. The west corner has the base of a round flanking tower about 9m in diameter, although the interior was square. The north corner has a tower of similar size but with a polygonal interior and traces of an apsidal projection towards the field. In the middle of the curtain between these two is a gateway flanked by two D-shaped towers 8m in diameter. Projecting from them is the abutment of a turning bridge, and then beyond, perched on the outer rampart, are foundations of a barbican probably of mid 13th century date, also with twin round towers flanking the gateway.

The southern end of the court is narrower, since whilst the western end of the SW side rises directly from a rock outcrop at the bottom of the ditch, beyond the rectangular tower the curtain is set back on top of a steep bank. At the south corner is a tower 8m in diameter containing a vaulted room below another chamber which had doorways leading out onto narrow berms between the curtain wall and the ditch slope. These berms must have been enclosed by palisades, there being posterns to other berms beyond the NW and NE curtain walls. Facing SE, very close to the east corner, is the lower part of a gatehouse 10m square with pilaster buttresses on the outer corners and a portcullis groove. This part may be earlier than the rest. In front are the late 13th century abutments for a counterbalanced drawbridge. Little remains of an early 14th century hall 23m long by 15m wide against the SW curtain. To roof over such a width would have necessitated timber arcades. The hall had a buttery and pantry at the south end and a kitchen extended from them to the gatehouse.

The keep at Helmsley

Helmsley Castle

The lord's private apartments were contained in a rectangular tower 14m by 12m adjoining the west corner of the hall. This tower was mostly rebuilt c1300, the SW wall then being provided with three buttresses and windows with seats at courtyard level and in the room below which was then given a ribbed vault. Latrines are provided in the south corner. The upper parts were again remodelled in the 1580s with mullion-and-transom windows and new fireplaces, the building then having five storeys and a low-pitched roof within a plain parapet. The two storey range 10m wide beyond this tower remains roofed and floored and contains exhibitions. A blocked doorway of c1200 suggests that this may have been the original hall block, but most of the features, including mullion-and-transom windows and plaster ceilings, are of the 1580s. Extending from here to the west corner of the court are footings of bakehouses and brewhouses, with several ovens. Only footings remain of a wall built from the west tower to the chapel to close off the SE end of the court as a more private space for the lord's family.

On the NE side of the court a U-shaped tower 17m by 15m straddles the line of the curtain. The apsed outer end of the building was destroyed down to its base when the castle was slighted. This building is usually known as the keep but in its original form it contained just a lofty chapel over a vaulted basement, with a spiral stair between them in the west corner. The chapel had three lancets facing the court and was reached by a doorway, now blocked, on the NW side. In the early 14th century the tower was heightened and provided with square turrets on the west and south corners, which still stand to the full height, with the parapet between them. The turrets have thin pilaster buttresses. In the remodelling the chapel and its roof space became two separate storeys, both vaulted, and a fourth storey was added with a fireplace on the NW side. The chapel had already been superseded by a detached rectangular chapel with angle buttresses built closeby to the west. This may have been the chapel consecrated in 1246. It in turn was later turned into a habitable space with a fireplace at the east end.

At the SE end of the castle is a large mid 13th century barbican in the form of a court 60m by 40m extending across the ditch and onto a widened portion of the outer rampart, where there are D-shaped towers at each end of a curtain preserved almost to full height, and a twin-towered gatehouse in the middle. Buildings were provided against the curtain here in the 14th century. The wing walls across the ditch seem to be later in date. That on the north has a small tower flanking the NE side of the main courtyard. The present frontage of the outer gatehouse passage dates from the 1580s. An outer ward beyond this barbican was never walled in stone.

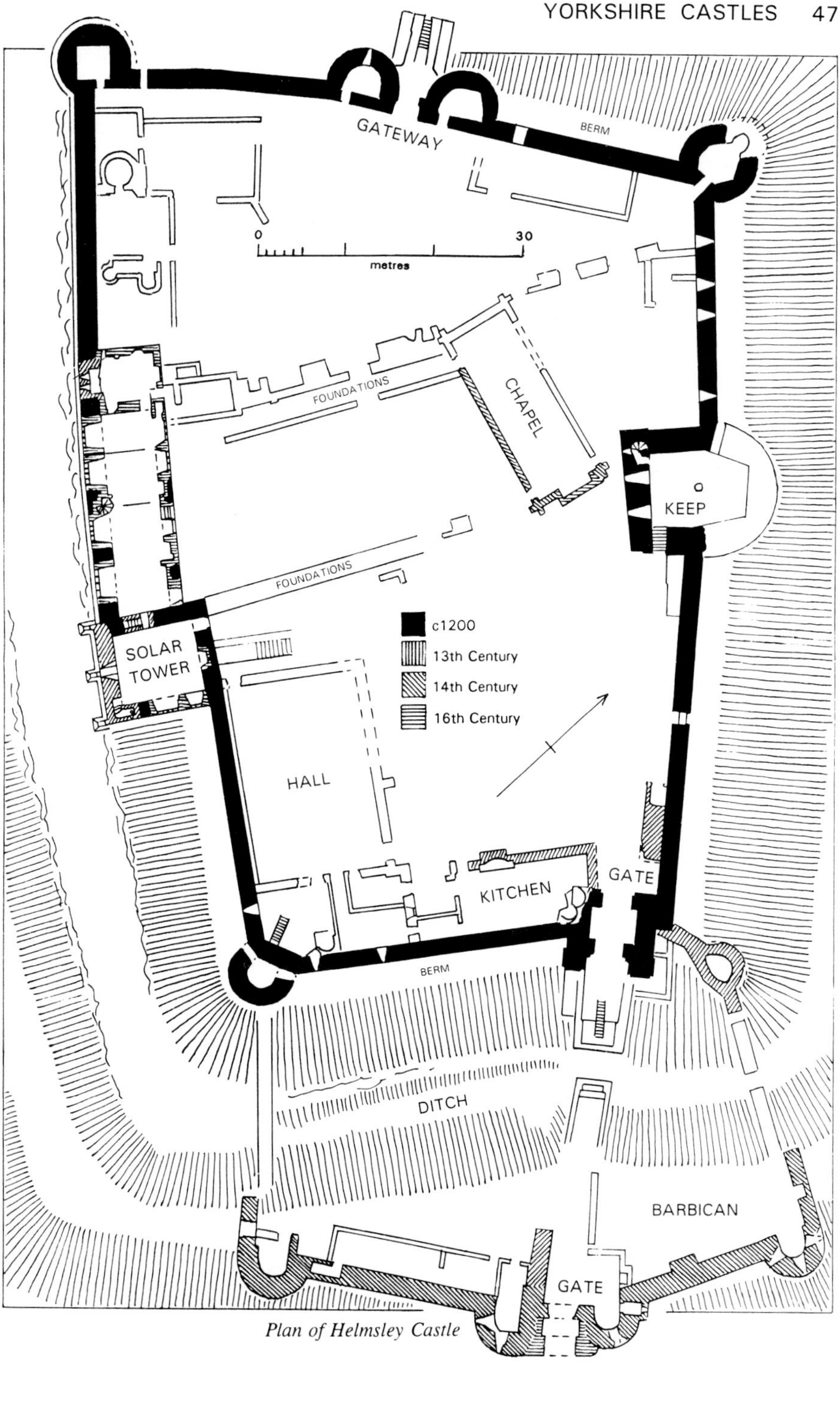

GATEWAY

BERM

0 30

metres

FOUNDATIONS

CHAPEL

KEEP

FOUNDATIONS

■ c1200
▥ 13th Century
▨ 14th Century
▤ 16th Century

SOLAR
TOWER

HALL

KITCHEN

GATE

BERM

DITCH

BARBICAN

GATE

Plan of Helmsley Castle

HOOD CASTLE   SE 504814

High up on Hood Hill a platform 5m high, 60m long and 30m wide has been formed by cutting ditches through a narrow ridge. There is a mention of the castle in 1218 in a context suggesting it was erected illegally at the end of King John's reign. In 1264 Henry III granted a licence for John de Eyvill to fortify "a place of his at La Hode, with a dyke and a wall of stone and lime and to crenellate it". The castle was sold to Thomas, Earl of Lancaster in 1319, but he immediately transferred it to John de Vesci. It is not mentioned after the death of Isabel de Vesci in 1334.

HOOTON PAGNELL HALL   SE 486078   V

Close to the Norman church is a fine ashlar-faced 14th century gatehouse with separate archways for carts and pedestrians. The top parts are partly 19th century but the corner oriel window is medieval. The main house contains Tudor panelling and an imported 17th century staircase but is not otherwise of interest.

HORNBY CASTLE   SE 226937   V

A tower house built by the St Quentin family in the late 14th century became the NW corner of a courtyard mansion erected by William Conyers, created Lord Conyers in 1506, his ancestor John, having married a St Quentin heiress in the early 15th century. The house was of two storeys with three storey corner towers. Elizabeth, heiress of the Conyers family, married Thomas Darcy and their son Conyers Darcy was made a lord by Charles I, whilst their grandson was made Earl of Holdernesse by Charles II in 1682. After the death of the 4th Earl Hornby passed via his heiress Amelia to Francis Godolphin. Their descendants the Osbornes, dukes of Leeds are still in possession. The entrance on the south side still has 15th century four-centred arches and side doorways and the tower in the SE corner has several early 16th century windows. The rest was remodelled c1800, and the upper parts of the east range and much of the west and north ranges, including the original tower house, disappeared in a mid 20th century remodelling.

Old print of Hornby Castle

Remains of the Beverley Gate at Hull

Howden Palace

HOWDEN PALACE   SE 749282   F

Adjoining the vicarage is a gateway bearing the arms of Bishop Langley of Durham (1406-37). In a park are reconstructed remnants of a second gatehouse at the north end of the formerly moated platform, measuring 60m by 36m, plus Bishop Skirlaw's great hall of 1388-1406 at the east end of the south range, now in a much altered state. It has a fine vaulted porch on the north side with Bishop Skirlaw's arms.

HULL CASTLE   TA 104286   F

In 1980 the lower part of the Beverley Gate of the town walls, demolished from 1776 onwards, was exposed and preserved. One of five gatehouses and several towers flanking the wall, this was the scene of Sir John Hotham's refusal to admit Charles I in 1642 which precipitated the Civil War. The town withstood two Royalist sieges later that year. The medieval town was strongly defended with the sea and the Humber protecting two sides of a rectangle and a late 14th century brick wall backed onto an earlier rampart and fronted by a water-filled ditch on the other two sides.

Excavations also revealed parts of a brick artillery fort which stood in the middle of a defensive rampart covering the harbour and having a trefoil-shaped blockhouse at each end. The fort was built by Henry VIII in 1541 and was square in plan with keel-shaped bastions set on two opposite sides and had a rectangular central tower about 22m by 12m. The entrance on the SW side was exposed along with a passage in the outer wall with a blocked gunport. The fort and the south blockhouse were incorporated into the huge triangular new citadel built by Charles II in the 1680s and demolished along with it in 1864. The north blockhouse was wrecked by the accidental explosion of a magazine during a Civil War siege and was removed in 1802. Traces of the south blockhouse were seen during building work in 1969-70.

Nothing remains of the moated house of the de la Poles, earls of Suffolk at Hull.

HUNMANBY CASTLE   TA 095775

This is a much damaged motte and bailey site. Hunmanby belonged to the Gants until 1294 and then passed to the Tattershalls, and finally ended up with the Percies.

HUTTON CONYERS   SE 326735

There are extensive earthworks which seem to have formed concentric moated enclosures, although they have been much mutilated. Part at least of these works may go back to King Stephen's reign, when Alan, Earl of Richmond, erected a castle here to threaten the town of Ripon. It was probably destroyed in 1154.

HUTTONS AMBO CASTLE   SE 763674

Above the north bank of the River Derwent is an embanked platform which in the 11th century was held by a Dane called Colswain in return for guard duties at the gateway of the castle at York. Excavations in the 1950s showed that the timber hall was later replaced in stone, as was the gate tower facing a causeway across the ditch. There was also eventually a curtain wall upon the rampart.

INGLEBY CASTLE   NZ 432129

Above the confluence of the Leven and the Tees is a motte with a 10m diameter summit about 2m above the level of a kidney-shaped bailey 40m by 35m with a shallow ditch 9m wide on the east side. The motte north side is damaged.

INGLEBY MANOR   NZ 586058

This is a late medieval courtyard house with a tower over the gateway on the north side. It was remodelled with new mullioned windows in the late 16th and 17th centuries and greatly altered in the 18th and 19th centuries.

KILDALE CASTLE   NZ 603095

In 1961 excavations revealed a structure 13.7m long by 8.8m long with ashlar faced walls 1.2m thick on the summit of a motte beside the station. The 19th century church lies on the site of a U-shaped bailey 50m across to the east, beyond which is a ditch. This castle was held by a junior branch of the Percy family. It was sold to the senior branch in 1502. A manor house here was leased to the Applebys c1560.

KILLERBY CASTLE   SE 258960

Incorporated into an outbuilding of Killerby Hall is a buttressed wall up to 1.2m thick which is thought to be a relic of a castle built by Sir Brian Fitz-Alan, who was granted a licence to crenellate by Edward I in 1291, having obtained the manor by marriage. On Sir Brian's death in 1306 it passed to John, Lord Grey, then to John, Lord Deincourt in 1387, and then in 1422 to the Lovels. Francis, Lord Lovel, forfeited by Henry VII in 1485, is recorded by Leland as having a castle at Killerby which had reverted to the Crown and was in ruins. It had been granted to Nicholas Kniston in 1487, and then went to Sir John Cuttes. The site may have had a wet moat.

To the NW at SE 254971 is the site of an older castle. The 3.5m high motte is much worn down but the bailey 57m across between it and the drop to the River Swale has a rampart 11m high at the SW corner. The western part of the site is ditched but the ditch does not continue along the south edge of the site.

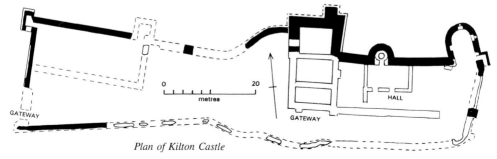

Plan of Kilton Castle

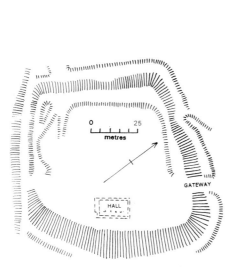

Plan of Huttons Ambo Castle

Kilton Castle

KILTON CASTLE   NZ 704177

This castle is thought to have been founded in the 1130s by Pagan Fitz-Walter but the curtain wall is thought to have been built c1160 by his son Osbert who later took the name de Kylton. His son or grandson William de Kylton remodelled the castle in the 1190s. Richard de Alta Ripa is thought to have rebuilt the west curtain and added the block near the gateway during the short space of time between when he inherited the castle in 1219 and his death in 1222, when it passed to the de Thweng family. By the 1340s the castle seems to have been lying empty and was regarded as of little value, but the Lumleys later leased (and then inherited) it. It was probably Sir Ralph Lumley, killed in a skirmish at Cirencester in 1400, who rebuilt the block of buildings between the two wards, filled in the ditch on the west side of them, and built a two storey hall block against the north side of the inner ward. Not long afterwards the family transferred to Lumley Castle in County Durham although a steward remained in occupation at Kilton. The castle was, however, just a "ruinous shell" by 1536, when George Lumley lost his estates for his part in the Pilgrimage of Grace. The Lloyds were in possession in the early 17th century , whilst in the 1660s Thomas Thweng is said to have removed much of the material to construct Kilton Hall. The estate passed through various hands subsequently. The ruins were repaired c1880 by the Whartons of Skelton and excavations were carried out from 1965 to 1975.

The ruins lie on a promontory with steep slopes down to a bend of the Kilton Beck. A ditch cuts off the promontory and prior to this are slight traces of an outer enclosure 100m by 60m with a ditch and rampart 2m high. On the promontory are two wards with a total length of 90m but nowhere wider than 30m and in fact the inner ward was only about 14m wide within the walls. Little remains of the south curtain and only footings remain of a composite block dividing the two wards. This block contained the inner gatehouse with a short section of curtain south of it, a probable kitchen to the north, and then beyond that a tower over 12m wide. A range along the north side of the inner ward contained the hall. Opening off it was a small well chamber in a round tower flanking the curtain. Projecting still further is a U-shaped tower of the mid 13th century containing several arrow-slits set at the east end of the north wall. The outer ward contained just one large building. Its northern corners have rectangular projections. The gateway south of it seems to have been a simple opening without any sort of tower.

Neville Castle at Kirkby Moorside

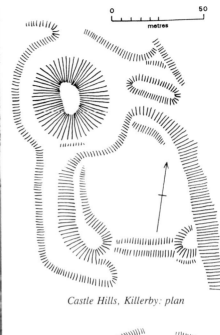

Castle Hills, Killerby: plan

Plan of Kippax Motte

KIMBERWORTH MOTTE   SK 405935

Nothing now remains of this probable motte and bailey castle.

KIPPAX: MANOR GARTH HILL   SE 417304

North of the church is a ringwork 30m across rising 3m above the ditch around the eastern half of the site. A hall, barn and oxhouse here are mentioned in 1341.

KIRKBY FLEETHAM   SE 285943

On the end of a low ridge is a quadrangular moated platform 55m across, presumably the site for which Henry le Scrope obtained a licence to crenellate from Edward II in 1314. There are indications that the moat was stone lined and about a hundred years ago a defaced section of wall 13m long still stood up to 4m high. The Scropes held the castle until 1630, by which time it had probably been abandoned.

KIRKBY KNOWLE CASTLE   SE 459874

A house called Newbuilding erected by James Danby in the 1650s, but incorporating parts of an early 16th century mansion built by Sir John Constable which was destroyed by fire in 1569, stands on the site of a mid 13th century castle with corner towers erected by Roger Lascelles. Inside is a stone with the date 1374.

KIRKBY MALZEARD CASTLE   SE 237745

This was one of the castles of Robert Mowbray, Earl of Northumberland which were forfeited to the Crown in 1095 after his rebellion. The slight remains suggest it was a motte and bailey site. It was destroyed by Henry II in 1174. The slight traces of masonry may be of later date.

KIRKBY MOORSIDE CASTLE   SE 695869

The quadrangular platform 80m by 60m with a 2m high rampart and ditch at SE 700868 is the site of a castle built in the 12th century by the Stuteville family. The manor later passed to the Wakes, who are thought to have built a hall block in the Manor Garth at the north end of the town. This site is now known as Neville Castle, since Ralph Neville, Earl of Westmorland is thought to have incorporated the older hall into a mansion about 70m long by 35m wide with four corner towers. Of it there remains only a a short and thin fragment of walling 6m high on the edge of a gully. When confiscated from Charles Neville, Earl of Westmorland after the rebellion in 1569 it was regarded as being too modest a house for an earl but suitable for a clergyman. The widow of the next earl, Henry, lived in the mansion until her death in 1595, after which it was probably abandoned. The manor was granted to the Villiers family, later dukes of Buckingham, but was sold in 1687 to the Duncombes, later lords Feversham. A toll-booth in the market place is said to have been built of materials taken from the ruins in the 18th century.

The King's Tower, Knaresborough

The King's Tower, Knaresborough   *Knaresborough Castle*

KNARESBOROUGH CASTLE   SE 349589   O

The Saxon name Chednaresberg used in Domesday Book suggests that the town may have once been enclosed with a bank and ditch, the word "burg" usually meaning a defensive enclosure. The first reference to a castle here is in 1129-30, when Henry I's Pipe Rolls record £11 being spent upon it by its custodian Eustace Fitz-John. In 1170 Hugh de Morville fled to his castle at Knaresborough after taking part in the murder of Archbishop Thomas Beckett in Canterbury Cathedral. Knaresborough was a favourite seat of King John, who liked to hunt in the forest there. He spent about £1,300 on the castle between 1203 and 1212, much of it going on the excavation of the deep ditch which isolated the accessible sides of the castle. By the end of his reign there must have been a stone curtain wall, although very little of it remains today, nor anything else so early apart from the ditch, but remains of a 12th century pillar were found under the floor of the later keep. The castle was garrisoned for King John against the rebel barons in 1215-6.

Court records of Edward I mention the White tower, the great hall, the great chamber, the great chapel, the chapel of St Thomas and the great gate. The D-shaped towers of the gateway date from late in his reign i.e. c1295-1305. The King's Tower or keep was built in 1307-12 by Edward II, although the castle had been nominally handed over in 1307 to his unpopular favourite Piers Gaveston. Excavations in 1990 showed that it replaced an earlier tower. In 1312 King Edward was in residence at Knaresborough whilst the barons besieged Scarborough Castle, in which Gaveston had taken refuge. He was executed after that castle surrendered. In 1317 John de Lilburn, a supporter of Thomas, Earl of Lancaster, seized the castle at Knaresborough. It was recaptured for Edward II three months later after a siege in which the curtain wall was breached. The Scots burnt the town during a raid in 1318, but the castle seems to have held out. In 1331 Knaresborough was given to Edward III's consort Queen Philippa as part of her marriage settlement. Until her death in 1369 she was frequently in residence.

In 1372 King Edward and Queen Philippa's fourth son, John of Gaunt, Duke of Lancaster was given Knaresborough as part of an exchange of lands. The castle became royal again when his son became Henry IV in 1399. In that year the deposed Richard II spent a night at Knaresborough before being taken off to captivity and death in Pontefract Castle. On the death of Henry V in 1422 Knaresborough was given in dower to his widow, Queen Catherine. It reverted to her son Henry VI when she died in 1437. From then on the castle served mainly as an administrative centre. Surveys of 1538 and 1561 note it as in need of some repair, and in the 1590s the upper storey of the 13th century courthouse was rebuilt by Sir Henry Slingsby, who had taken a lease of the site. The castle held a Royalist garrison until it surrendered in December 1644 to a Parliamentary force after a siege of four months which culminated in the curtain wall being breached with cannon. An order for demolition in 1648 was probably not acted on until 1648. The curtain wall was then demolished but the court house was left in use and the King's Tower got a last minute reprieve after the townsfolk petitioned for it to be spared to provide a prison.

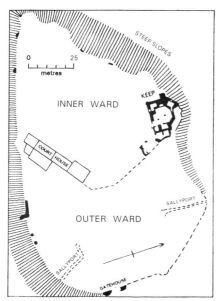

Plan of Knaresborough Castle

Knaresborough Castle

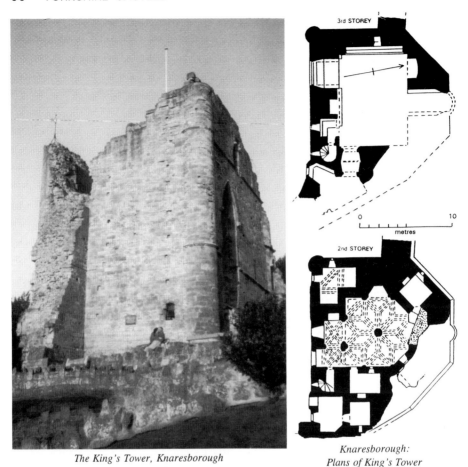

The King's Tower, Knaresborough

Knaresborough:
Plans of King's Tower

The castle stands on the west side of the town above a steep drop to the River Nidd. King John's great ditch still remains on the south side but has been filled in on the east. It isolated a platform 110m long by 70m wide which has been a public park since the District Council leased the site from Queen Victoria in 1888. The courthouse, now a museum, lies on the site of the southern half of a cross-wall which curved round from it to the King's Tower to divide off an inner ward on the point of the promontory. The courthouse has typical mullioned windows of the 1590s and contains original court furniture of that period, but the basement is probably 13th century, whilst one doorway is 14th century. A prison was added at the east end in the 18th century on the site of a medieval chapel, and there is a later extension at the west end. Fragments of two turrets remain on the south side of the inner ward and east of the courthouse is a fragment of the White Lady Tower, part of which stood 7.5m high until it fell in 1940. Facing east are two solid semi-circular ashlar-faced towers 5m in diameter and 10m high added probably in the 1290s against the now-lost curtain wall to flank the outer gateway. The arch between the towers collapsed in 1847. An unusual feature of the outer ward are two tunnels hewn through solid rock down to sallyports opening onto the bottom of the ditch.

The King's Tower of 1307-12 measures 18m by 15m over walls up to 4m thick. Intended as a majestic and secure residence it stands on the north side at the junction of the inner and outer ward walls. The building has an unusual plan with the part projecting to the field being semi-octagonal with a small round projection rising from the outermost face. A drawing of 1538 shows oriel windows in this projection at two upper levels and also depicts a north-facing gatehouse into the outer ward immediately east of the King's Tower. There was a complex ceremonial approach up steps from a porch between the crosswall between the wards, then under a portcullis to an anteroom in the SE corner and then another passage, also protected by a portcullis, led into the audience chamber. The anteroom had a window with seating facing the inner ward. The audience chamber has a huge arch in the west wall which framed a dais on which a throne could be mounted. The dais was lighted by large three-light window in a deep embrasure decorated with ball-flowers and fitted with seats in the south wall. There was another window embrasure in the north wall. Both these walls contain fireplaces, that on the north heating the dais.

From the SE corner of the audience chamber there is access to a spiral stair (with the unusual feature of a stone handrail) down to a room below with a fireplace and a fine rib-vault supported on a central octagonal pier. This room served either as a kitchen or as a lodging for an official. It has its own doorway to the inner ward, and access to a mural room on the east side, and another room facing NW which contains a latrine, although the chamber is wider than needed for that purpose and it has been suggested that it could have contained a bathtub. At this level the SW corner of the building, which has a small round turret of slight projection, contains a vaulted L-shaped strong-room reached direct from the court. Two rooms in the SE corner were probably a porter's lodging, since they open off the court. Yet another doorway from the court leads onto steps down to a rib-vaulted cellar with a central pier. The spiral stair also continued up to the bedroom on the topmost storey, now much ruined, but with evidence of a single wide window in each of the north and south walls. There was probably a chapel in the wall thickness on the now-destroyed east side of the building at that level.

LAUGHTON-EN-LE-MORTHEN: CASTLE HILL   SK 516882   V

West of the church is a kidney-shaped bailey 60m long with a rampart and ditch. On the SW side is a motte rising 9m to a summit 9m across. Laughton formed part of the Honour of Tickhill held by Roger de Busli at the time of Domesday Book.

LECONFIELD MOAT   TA 013432

A large moat remains on a site which Edward II licensed Henry, Lord Percy to fortify in 1308. The house is thought to have been rebuilt by a later Henry Percy, 5th Earl of Northumberland c1500. Set around a rectangular court were three storey rectangular corner towers and two storey ranges which had timber-framed inner walls, It was demolished in 1608-9.

LOCKINGTON CASTLE   SE 998465

There are slight traces of a bailey to the east of a wet-moated ringwork about 45m across on top with the rampart rising 4m above the moat water level. See p4.

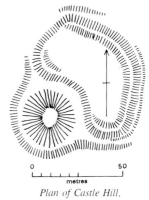

0   50
metres

Plan of Castle Hill,
Laughton-en-le-Morthen

MALTON CASTLE   SE 790716

On the end of a ridge are the overgrown and slight remains of a motte. In 1138 it was handed over to the Scots by Eustace Fitz-John but was soon captured and burnt by Archbishop Thurstan. A mention of pick-men being employed when the castle was destroyed by King John in 1214 suggests that the rebuilding c1160 by William de Vesci (son of Eustace) was in stone. In 1251 John and Agnes de Vesci founded a chantry in the chapel. There is a mention of the "old Gate" of the castle in a late 13th century charter. The castle passed in 1315 to Gilbert de Ayton, but his possession was disputed until 1318. During that period Edward II visited the castle and allowed one of the Comyns to live in it, whilst in 1317 there was an unsuccessful attempt by the king to give it to John de Mowbray. The castle was captured and destroyed by the Scots after their victory at Byland in 1322 and by Leland's time there was only a farmhouse on the site. In 1611 Ralph, Lord Eure built a mansion on the site, but after a dispute over possession it was demolished for its materials in 1675. Three archways still survived either from this building or the earlier castle until demolished in 1858. Nothing remains of a rampart of uncertain date around the town.

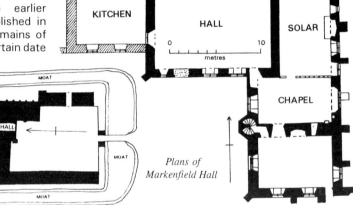

Plans of Markenfield Hall

Markenfield Hall

Markenfield Hall

MARKENFIELD HALL SE 295673

Edward II granted a licence for the crenellation of this building to his Chancellor of the Exchequer John de Markenfield. Much of what still stands in a little-altered state is thought to date from before John's death in 1323. The Markenfields were forfeited by Queen Elizabeth for their part in the rebellion of 1569 and the house was sold by the queen to Sir Thomas Egerton. He added the present gatehouse and made a few other alterations. Sir Fletcher Norton, created 1st Baron Grantley of Markenfield on his retirement as Speaker of the House of Commons in 1783, purchased the house from the Egertons. He made considerable repairs to the decayed roofs. Further alterations were carried out by the 4th Lord Grantley in the 1850s but no other work of importance was done between then and the renovations of the 1980s except for the southern half of the east range being converted into a farmhouse in 1960.

The mansion lies on a platform about 60m by 50 surrounded by a wet moat about 8m wide, except on the south, where it is much wider. At a distance of about 60m away there was formerly an outer moat of similar width, now filled in. There are ranges around the west, north and east sides of the court but the primary buildings form an L-shaped group around the NE corner. They consist of a hall 12.8m by 8.8m with a solar to the east, south of which is a chapel with another chamber beyond, all of these being set over rib-vaulted undercrofts with central piers and later windows facing the court. West of the hall is a kitchen extending through two storeys. The hall doorway once had a porch in front of it. The north and south walls each contain a pair of two-light windows with seats in the embrasures and there is a large fireplace on the north side. A doorway in the hall SE corner leads to the chapel, off which there was access to the solar and the south chamber. The latter has a spiral stair leading down in a polygonal turret facing the court, whilst the solar has a latrine turret projecting to the north and a fireplace between the east-facing windows. The chapel has a three-light east window and a squint through from the south chamber.

MELSONBY TOWER   NZ 201083

The slight remains are of small tower house of perhaps even a chapel.

MEXBOROUGH: CASTLE HILL   SK 127876   F

The circular bailey 48m across has a rampart rising 5m above its ditch. This part may have been a ringwork before the addition of the 6m high motte to the SW. Little is now visible of a small enclosure in the a rc entrant angle between the two parts.

MIDDLEHAM CASTLE   SE 127876   E

The original castle site here was the earthwork higher up 450m south of the stone castle. Known as William's Hill, it comprises an oval motte rising 11m from the surrounding ditch to a summit 55m by 40m, with a kidney shaped bailey 65m by 30m to the SE (see page 5). It is assumed to have been erected by Ribald, who was granted an estate here in 1086 by his brother Alan the Red, lord of Richmond. The great keep on the lower site was built either by Ribald's son Ralph, who died in 1168, or the latter's son Robert, who died c1184. When their descendant Ralph Fitz-Ranulph died in 1270 Middleham passed to his daughter Mary, who married Robert Neville of Raby. The chapel on the east side of the keep was added shortly afterwards and then a few years later a curtain wall was added around the keep.

Keep and chapel block at Middleham

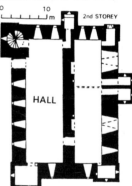

Middleham: plan of keep

Middleham Castle

Middleham Castle

Ralph Neville was created Earl of Westmorland by Richard II in 1397 and in the early 15th century he remodelled the castle on the lines of nearby Bolton with ranges around the court. Ralph's daughter Cecily married Richard, Duke of York and became the mother of Edward IV and Richard III. Cecily's brother Richard not only became 2nd Earl of Westmorland but also, by marrying the heiress, obtained the earldom of Salisbury. After the Duke of York was killed and defeated in battle by Henry VI's consort Margaret at Wakefield in 1460 Salisbury was captured and executed. His son Richard also obtained a second earldom, that of Warwick, by another fortuitous marriage. He helped put Edward IV on the throne in 1461 but eventually fell out with him. After an attempt to re-instate Henry VI (for which history has labelled him Warwick the Kingmaker) he was defeated and killed at the battle of Barnet in 1471. Middleham was then given by Edward IV to his brother Richard, Duke of Gloucester who was married to Warwick's daughter Anne. It was used by Duke Richard as his principal seat in his function as Edward IV's lieutenant of the north. The north range may be of this period, and perhaps the clerestory of the hall in the keep.

After Edward IV died in 1483 his brother took the throne as Richard III. Even when suspicions began to mount about what had become of his nephews, the Princes in the Tower, Richard remained popular in Yorkshire. His only son, Edward, who had been born at Middleham, died in the castle in 1484. With Richard III's defeat and death at Bosworth in 1485 the castle passed to Henry VII. When James I gave it to Sir Henry Lindley in 1604 it had not been occupied for over a century and was ruinous. Sir Henry made part of it habitable, dying in the castle in 1610, and it was still occupied by the Edward, Lord Loftus in 1644. Parliament ordered the castle to be "rendered untenable" in 1646 and the east curtain may then have been destroyed, along with most of the parapets. The castle was sold in 1662 to the Woods, who owned it until it was sold in 1889. It has been in state guardianship since 1925.

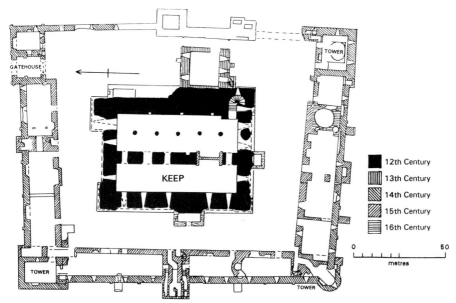

Plan of Middleham Castle

The stone castle measures 65m by 53m and has a ditch 9m wide still remaining on the north and east, although it has been filled in on the other sides. The early 14th century curtain wall was a flimsy affair only 1.3m thick and 5m high to the wall-walk, a dramatic contrast to the massive keep, which has walls over 3m thick. In its heightened 15th century form, strengthened by various turrets and buttresses, the outer wall stands almost complete on the north, west and south sides, but little more than foundations remain on the east side. There are footings there of a gatehouse open towards a vanished outer court (now partly built over) which in 1538 contained stables and workshops mostly in decay. The base of a latrine turret further south is probably 15th century. At the SW corner is a D-shaped tower 4.8m in diameter externally, originally just an open bastion the same height as the main wall-walk, but later enclosed at the back and then heightened by two storeys and provided with an adjoining spiral staircase. The other three corners have rectangular towers, that at the SE corner being of just two storeys. The other towers were remodelled in the 15th century, that at the NW corner being heightened and widened, whilst the other was provided with a new vaulted gatehall and an upper storey with diagonal buttresses and a machicolated parapet on the north and east sides.

In the 15th century the curtain wall was raised and on the south side a range 6m wide internally was added to provide apartments over service rooms, latrines being provided in a turret added to the curtain. The central lower room was a brewhouse with a large oven. A horse-operated mill was constructed in it in the 16th century. On the upper storey at the west end was the "Lady Chamber", which was connected by a wooden gallery to the presence chamber in the keep. A narrow range of two storeys was also added against the west side of the court. Here both levels were originally habitable spaces with fireplaces and latrines provided in a central tower 5.5m wide and two intermediate buttresses, but a bakehouse was later inserted at the south end and the lower rooms then vaulted over. Above the bakehouse lay the nursery. A turret rises over the spiral stair in the SE corner of the latrine tower.

The late 14th century NW tower was originally 10m long by 6.8m wide, but the width was increased on the east side to 9m in the 15th century. It contained three storeys, the upper rooms having fireplaces and latrines. The gatehouse at the NE corner measures 12.4m by 7.4m and contained two storeys of pairs of upper rooms over a vaulted gatehall flanked by a guard room. The inner arch of the gateway passage has a portcullis groove. The lower part has thin angle buttresses from which rise diagonal corner turrets. The machicolated parapets on the north and east sides were once probably adorned with the figures of armed men found during excavations. The apartments along the north side of the keep were built in the 15th century and provided a lodging of several rooms for an official known as the auditor. There is a latrine projection, behind which is cross-wall containing a spiral staircase. As with the other ranges the inner wall is mostly destroyed to within a metre of courtyard level.

The keep measures 31m by 23.5m above a battered plinth almost obliterated by stone robbing and was one of the largest of its type in England. A long flight of steps against the north wall led up to a doorway into the NE corner of the hall, which measured about 25m by 8m and must have had a fireplace in the centre of the floor. In the 15th century the lighting of the hall was improved by provided a clerestory, which on the east side lies within the old wall-walk. Adjacent to the entrance is a doorway to a very wide spiral stair rising from the cellar below the hall up to the wall-walks. This stair lies in a large and boldly projecting corner turret rising high above the rest of the building. There are similar but slightly smaller turrets projecting to the north and containing chambers at the NE and NW corners (the first of these is a vaulted chapel), whilst the SW corner has a more conventional clasping buttress of shallow projection. The cellar under the hall had a groin vault two bays wide supported on a row of five circular piers. To the west of a 2.7m thick cross-wall lay the private chamber at the north end and the presence chamber at the south end. Below them was another vaulted cellar lighted by five loops with stepped cills facing west. In later years the southern end was provided with a large fireplace in the cross-wall to convert it into a kitchen and there is a well at the north end. Turrets containing latrines were later added to the south and west side to provide the upper chambers with latrines, although the western latrines probably west out of use after a bridge was built from the private chamber to the top storey of the central latrine tower of the outer west curtain wall. The private chamber has a large 15th century window replacing two of the original Norman ones. To the east of the keep is a very ruined late 13th century block which contained a vaulted chapel on the third storey, with a priest's lodging in the two vaulted storeys below.

MIRFIELD CASTLE   SE 211204

The church of 1871 lies on the bailey platform of a motte lying immediately NW of it, and the tower remaining from the medieval church lies at a lower level to the SE. The motte rises 9m above a ditch 2m deep to a summit 18m across. Originally held by tenants of the de Lacys, Mirfield was later a seat of the Nevilles. By Henry VIII's reign the castle had been superseded by a timber framed house where Castle Hall now lies.

Mirfield Castle: plan

MOUNT FERRANT CASTLE   SE 795639

This narrow promontory was divided by ditches into three wards. In the 1170s Henry II agreed to the destruction of the castle to punish its teenage lord William Fossard, after his illicit affair with the sister of his guardian William le Gros, Count of Aumale.

Mortham Tower

MORTHAM TOWER   NZ 087142

The hall on the north side of the court, the great chamber
west of it and a block extending north from the great
chamber are 14th century, built in replacement of an older
house on the other side of the Greta destroyed by the
Scots. The ashlar-faced status symbol tower added in the
late 15th century by Thomas Rokeby provided extra
private rooms. It measures 8m by 6m and has bartizans
alternately round and polygonal with a stair turret on the
NE corner. At parapet level the bartizans have unglazed
rectangular windows. The west wing and the low curtain
wall and gatehouse on the south side are of c1500. The
east wing also appears to be mostly of that date. The
great chamber was remodelled in the late 16th century.
The family later lived at Rokeby Hall, the hall block at
Mortham being made into a barn c1830. The house later
became derelict but was restored to domestic use c1939.

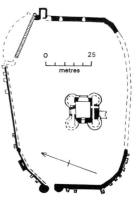

Plan of Mulgrave Castle

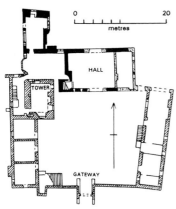

Plan of Mortham Tower

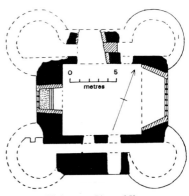

Mulgrave: Plan of Keep

The keep at Mulgrave

Tower at Mulgrave

MULGRAVE CASTLE   NZ 839117

The castle consists of a very ruined tower keep standing near the middle of an oval court 80m from east to west by 60m wide lying on a wooded ridge. The 13th century curtain wall was poorly built with weak mortar and has required much rebuilding and propping up at various period with buttresses. On the south side the wall has gone and on the north side it is no more than a thin parapet on a retaining wall with later buttresses. The east wall has two deep recesses and from it projects a 14th century turret about 4.2m square containing a small room. North of the turret a straight 16th century section of wall cuts off the former NE corner which must have collapsed. Facing west was a gateway flanked by solid round turrets 5m in diameter, one of which recently collapsed. There are many later medieval buttresses here.

The keep measures about 15.3m by 14.5 over walls up to 3.6m thick. Some 13th century masonry appears to survive on the south side, where there are traces of an added porch, but the keep was rebuilt in the early 14th century and given four round corner towers about 7m in diameter over walls 1.5m thick, of which little now remains. The rooms in the southern towers were reached from an entrance passage. The seven light mullioned window in the east wall and the smaller similar windows facing north and west formed part of a late 16th century remodelling.

The castle may have been built by Peter de Maulay after his marriage to a Turnham heiress of the estate in 1220. Until then the seat of the estate was Foss Castle, a ringwork 3m high and 35m across with a bailey 60m by 45m, backing onto a ravine at NZ 832117, and probably erected by Nigel Fossard in the 1070s. The towers of the keep may date from 1326 when the fourth Peter de Maulay was ordered by Edward II to go north from his other seat at Folkingham in Lincolnshire to occupy and fortify the castle, which was described as ruinous in 1309. After the widow of the sixth Peter Maulay died in 1428 Mulgrave passed to the Bigods. Sir Francis Bigod was forfeited for his part in the Pilgrimage of Grace but his widow remained in residence in the castle until 1566, after which it passed to her grandson Francis Radcliffe. On his death Queen Elizabeth granted the castle to Edmund, Lord Sheffield, Lord President of the North under James I, and created Earl of Mulgrave by Charles I in 1626. Despite his support for Parliament the castle held a Royalist garrison until it surrendered in June 1644. It was then used as a prison until dismantled in 1647, the 2nd Earl being paid £1,000 as compensation. In the 18th century the ruin passed to Henry Phipps, created Earl of Mulgrave in 1812.

Nappa Hall

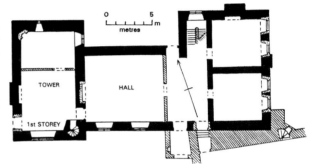

Interior of Paull Holme Tower

Plan of Nappa Hall

NAPPA HALL   SD 966907

This 15th century building consists of a central hall with a solar wing to the west and a two storey wing to the east beyond the screens passage. The hall has a pair of two-light windows and a porch on the south side. The east wing is embattled and contains bedrooms over what were once a kitchen and buttery, the upper rooms being reached by a modern staircase in the NW corner. The solar lies on the lowest level of a block carried up through four storeys to a parapet and turret over the staircase in the SE corner. Although impressive, this block was not really defensible since the windows in the south end are largest at ground level and smaller at the higher levels. The reverse of this might be expected in a defensible building. The L-shaped block with a re-entrant angle facing SE added to the SE corner of the main building was added c1637 and is said to have formed until 1671 a separate dwelling for Thomas, younger brother of James Metcalf, who occupied the main building. This added block contains the existing kitchen at the south end.

NORTHALLERTON CASTLE   SE 362942

Construction of the North Eastern Railway and its branch to Leyburn has removed most of the remains of a ringwork 120m across and a bailey east of it probably erected by William I and granted by William II to the Bishop of Durham. In 1141 it was captured and strengthened by William Comyn, the usurping Bishop of Durham. Bishop Hugh de Puiset garrisoned the castle for King William of Scotland in 1174 but was compelled to surrender it to Henry II, by whom it was destroyed in 1176. The site was used as a camping ground by the Earl of Surrey's army on its way north to victory at Flodden in 1513, and by the Duke of Cumberland's army in 1745.

North of the town, at SE 365940, (to the east of the other site) a cemetery lies on the site of a second castle with traces of a low motte and a bailey with a ditch 18m wide. This site was probably fortified by Hugh de Puiset, Bishop of Durham, in c1177 to replace the other site. A new palisade or peel was built around it by the carpenter Adam de Glasham in 1314 as a defence against Scottish raids following the English defeat at Bannockburn. According to Leland the Bishop of Durham then had a strong palace here "well moated". In 1664 Bishop John Cosin allowed stones from the ruined palace to be used to repair the castle mills, which stood nearby. A fragment of the gatehouse stood until c1700 but the remains were plundered for building materials by the townsfolk during the 18th century.

NORTON TOWER   SD 976571

Three thin ruined walls of a tower of late date lie on the west side of Rylstone Fell.

section

3rd STOREY

PAULL HOLME TOWER   TA 185249

This fine late 15th century brick structure is adorned with Tudor roses and the arms of the Holmes and Wastneys, who intermarried c1400. It is complete except for the roof and topmost floor, and formed the solar block of a timber framed hall lying to the south. The tower measures 10.7m by 8m at the level of the vaulted basement, where the walls are 1.5m thick but they are reduced by external offsets above. The parapet at the summit is corbelled out but without machicolations. Both the cellar and the principal room above have numerous recesses in the walls. From one of these opens a machicolation defending the entrance doorway at ground level, which has a drawbar slot. The private room currently only has one two-light window in the far end wall from that containing the stairs and a latrine, but originally there must have been others. The third storey is also poorly provided with windows. The Holmes had a seat here by the 14th century.

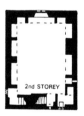

2nd STOREY

1st STOREY

Paull Holme: plans

Paull Holme Tower

PICKERING CASTLE   SE 798845   E

This castle was founded by William I during his campaign of 1069-70 in northern England. Henry I issued a charter from the castle in 1108 and perhaps was the builder of the Old Hall. The 4m high ringwork 30m across on Beacon Hill at SE 793845 measuring 33m by 24m was probably a siegework erected to threaten the castle during the anarchy of the 1140s under King Stephen. The Pipe Rolls record expenditure on the castle by Henry II, and his sons Richard and John. The bridge mentioned in the 1180s was presumably a drawbridge at the inner ward entrance and the circuit of the inner ward wall is thought to be of that period. The castle seems to have been damaged during the civil war of the first years of Henry III's reign. In 1220 a jury enquired into what condition the castle was in before Geoffrey de Nevill, Sheriff of Yorkshire, began supervising repairs. The several hundred pounds spent between 1218 and 1226 seems to have gone on a complete rebuild of the keep, the original having been presumably destroyed in the war, the construction of the new hall and the repair of the inner ward wall. In 1225 there is the first record of the arrangement (probably going back to the 11th century) under which the tenants of the Honour of Pickering were each required to maintain a length of the palisade of pointed stakes called the herisson which then still enclosed the outer ward.

There are several records of oaks being taken from the adjacent forest for work at the castle in the 1250s. In the early 1260s the castle was fortified by the Justiciar, Hugh Bigod for the king in the struggles against Simon de Montfort. In 1267 Henry granted the Honour of Pickering to his younger son Edmund, along with the earldom of Lancaster. A survey at Edmund's death in 1296 described the castle as weak and of little value. However, his son Thomas garrisoned the castle during his struggles against Edward II which led to his defeat and execution in 1322, and in 1314 the new hall was remodelled to provide a residence for Thomas's wife, the heiress Alice de Lacy. The castle was threatened by the Scots during their campaign of 1322, the invaders being bought off by the town and hostages taken, including the castle constable. In 1323 Edward II visited the castle and ordered the new constable, John de Kilvington, to repair the buildings and replace the herisson palisade of the outer ward with a stone curtain with towers.

The chapel at Pickering

Site of the Constable's lodgings, Pickering

Edward III returned the castle to Thomas's brother Henry, whose son Henry was created Duke of Lancaster in 1351. The title died with him but was revived for John of Gaunt, Edward's fourth son, who married the duke's heiress Blanche. The castle became a Crown possession again in 1399 when their son took the throne as Henry IV. The castle continued to be maintained during the 15th century, the two drawbridges, the constable's buildings, the stables, and the chapel roof all being repaired or rebuilt in the 1440s. A survey of 1537 mentions the stables and the wall of the outer ward, plus the new hall and chapel as being in good repair but there were no munitions in the castle and the rest of it was in decay, the keep being described as "evil rent, riven and perished". The constable, Sir Richard Cholmley, removed materials from the castle to build a new mansion at Roxby and by 1565 the castle was in a poor condition. Another survey in 1621 found the building quite ruinous except for the Mill Tower, which served as a prison, and the chapel, which was then used as a courthouse since the new hall was a ruin. The Duchy of Lancaster had the chapel re-roofed in the 19th century and consolidation of the ruins began after they were handed over to State care in 1926.

Coleman Tower and motte at Pickering

Diate Hill Tower

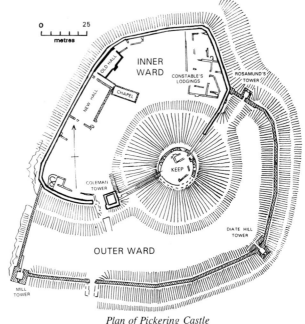

Plan of Pickering Castle

The castle lies on the north side of the town and has a drop to the Pickering Beck on the west side. The inner ward is an elongated oval of 115m by 65m. Its curtain wall is much defaced and broken down, especially towards the SW end, where the remains of ovens mark the site of the kitchens and other service buildings, probably timber-framed. On the NW side are the remains of the new hall, which was 23m long by 12m wide internally. It had an upper floor, the private chamber being at the north end. Beyond is a passage to the chapel and the much smaller and originally free-standing old hall, where there remains a Norman arch in the curtain wall. The chapel, dating from the 1220s, with original lancets on each side, and still roofed, adjoins the new hall eastern corner. A chantry of St Mary founded by Edward IV in the 1460s was abolished by Henry VIII in 1547.

In the eastern part of the inner ward are foundations of the constable's lodgings, probably timber framed. The only tower on the circuit of the inner ward wall was the Coleman Tower, a square structure straddling the wall beside the gateway. In 1323 its basement was used as a prison. The tower was then remodelled and given a new parapet. From there was access to the "Grayss Chamber", from which the inner gateway drawbridge was operated, and later used as a records room. Steps lead up beside the tower onto the curtain wall leading up the west side of the motte to the keep. The motte summit measures about 20m across and bears fragmentary remains of a shell keep, nominally circular, although the wall is facetted, and containing foundations of timber-framed buildings. On the north the shell wall still stands to the height of the wall-walk about 4m above the inside and is pierced by two arrow loops. Originally there were about eight or nine of them. This is the only example of a shell keep having arrow-loops below the level of the wall-walk parapet. On the east are traces of a latrine within a thickening of the wall. The entrance shows no signs of defensive arrangements so the keep and the steps up to it must have been treated as one defensive unit. The well in the motte ditch was originally over 20m deep.

The outer ward takes the form of a platform up to 25m wide beyond the ditch around the inner ward and motte base. Much of its wall and towers are fairly well preserved apart from the loss of parts of the parapet and the destruction of the outer parts of the gatehouse. On the west the wall is built up from a rocky outcrop on the side of the gorge of the beck and was probably never much higher than it is now. The Mill Tower at this corner measures 8m square and contains a basement prison (the door was fastened from the outside) and just one upper room reached by an external stair. A horse-operated mill is thought to have stood nearby. Facing SE is the 6m square Diate Hill Tower, which contained two upper rooms over a basement. External stairs led to an upper doorway and from there a spiral stair led up to the thinly-walled best room at the top, a lodging for an official with a latrine, wall cupboards and a later two-light window. Between here and the gatehouse lay the stables, which from the evidence of old surveys seem to have had a timber-framed upper storey (probably accommodation for grooms) over a stone lower storey. The basement of Rosamund's Tower forms a postern leading out of the inner ward ditch. There are again two upper rooms. This building rose higher than the inner ward wall ever did so after its construction the inner ward cannot have been separately defensible, although a turret was built at the junction of the two wall-walks to control access between them.

PICKHILL CASTLE   SE 346838

A 4m high mound 30m by 40m on top was absorbed into a railway embankment in 1851. Traces of a bailey remained on the west until the early 20th century. The site lies by the Pickhill Beck, west of the church. Probably built in the 1140s by Roald de Ennase, the castle passed by marriage to the Nevilles c1190. King John ordered it destroyed in 1216 but he died before it could be carried out and the site probably remained occupied until destroyed during a Scottish raid c1319.

Rosamund's Tower at Pickering

The keep at Pontefract

Gascoigne Tower at Pontefract

PONTEFRACT CASTLE   SE 460224   F

Pontefract was the centre of a lordship of 162 manors granted by William I to Ilbert de Lacy c1076. He probably founded the castle immediately and it is mentioned in the Domesday survey of 1086. His son Robert was forfeited by Henry I in 1106 and Pontefract was granted first to Hugh de Laval and then William Maltravers. The latter was murdered in 1135 and King Stephen then returned Pontefract to Ilbert II de Lacy, who was succeeded by his brother Henry in 1141. It was probably Henry and his son Robert, who succeeded in 1177, who enclosed the inner bailey with a stone wall with several square towers. Robert was succeeded in 1194 by his aunt's great-grandson Roger Fitz-Eustace who then adopted the de Lacy surname. Roger only obtained possession of the castle on the accession of King John, since Richard I had retained it for his own use. The stone keep was either begun by Roger after his return from duty in 1201-4 as commander of Chateau Gaillard, or by his son John, perhaps in the 1230s after he was created Earl of Lincoln by Henry III. The last of this line was John's grandson Henry, who died in 1311, his heir having drowned in the well of the fine castle he was erecting at Denbigh in North Wales.

Earl Henry left a daughter Alice who was married to Thomas, Earl of Lancaster. He is thought to have improved the castle. After Earl Thomas was defeated and executed in 1322 Edward II took possession of the castle and carried out some work upon it, including the construction of a new tower. Shortly after his accession in 1327 the young Edward III returned Pontefract to Thomas's brother Henry. When his son Henry, Duke of Lancaster died in 1361 the castle and honour passed via his daughter Blanche to her husband John of Gaunt, fourth son of Edward III, by whom he was created Duke of Lancaster. In 1374 work began on heightening the keep, using stone quarried from the ditch around the bailey. The castle was garrisoned in 1382 when John of Gaunt fell out with his nephew Richard II. In 1399 Richard II banished John's son Henry Bolingbroke, but the latter returned and forced Richard to abdicate. Henry then took the throne and imprisoned Richard at Pontefract, where he died (or more likely was murdered) in 1400. The castle has belonged to the Crown ever since as part of the Duchy of Lancaster. Henry IV carried out a rebuilding of several of the towers and perhaps the domestic buildings. Henry VI repaired the great hall and barbican in 1439 and built a new larder in the 1440s. By 1609 the castle was decayed but Prince Charles had it repaired in 1618-20.

Pontefract Castle was held for King Charles during the Civil War and suffered three well documented sieges by Parliamentary troops. The first siege began on Christmas Day 1644. A heavy bombardment of the SW side resulted in the collapse of the Piper Tower but the main enciente remained impervious. The attackers then tried mining under the walls but since they were built upon rock faces (possibly then not exposed) this proved unsuccessful. Excavations in the kitchen area have found three shafts thought to have been dug by the defenders as countermines in order to detect by listening to (and intercept if need be) the attackers' tunnelling. The siege was raised at the beginning of March when a Royalist force under Sir Marmaduke Langdale arrived and defeated the attackers in a battle at Chequerfield.

By mid-March 1645 the castle was again under siege. No attempt was made to breach the defences, which were simply encircled by entrenchments to starve the garrison out. At first the defenders were able to go out foraging and in June they cut a trench from the east gate down to All Saints church as a covered way for that purpose. Two days later the attackers' siegeworks were completed and after a month the garrison agreed terms that allowed them to march out to Newark. The castle was then repaired and garrisoned by Parliamentary troops.

In 1648 the castle fell to a local Royalist rising led by Colonel John Morris. Cromwell was busy dealing with the threat posed by the Scottish army under the Duke of Hamilton, and although the castle was soon blockaded by Parliamentary troops it was some while before Cromwell and Lambert arrived to press the siege with vigour. A contemporary letter written by Cromwell acknowledges the castle as being one of the strongest in England, "well watered; situated on rock in every part of it; and therefore difficult to mine. The walls are very thick and high, with strong towers; and if battered, very difficult of access, by reason of the depth and steepness of the graft". The castle was again surrounded by a series of small forts, artillery emplacements and trenches. After nearly five months the garrison surrendered in late March 1649, two months after King Charles had been executed and long after all Royalist resistance elsewhere on the mainland had been quashed. Coins struck in the castle to pay the garrison still survive, the later ones acknowledging Charles II as king. Just three days after its fall Parliament ordered the defences to be destroyed, the work lasting several weeks and costing nearly £800. The only part to remain in use was the barbican, the guard house of which was used as a prison for debtors and offenders. French prisoners-of-war were kept within it in 1673. In the 18th century the corporation rented out the castle grounds to Dunhills for cultivating liquorice. In the 1880s the castle grounds first became a park and excavations began to be made.

The Norman castle comprised an egg-shaped bailey 120m by 95m occupying the whole summit of a low hill with a motte at the south end. In the late 14th century an outer bailey 60m wide and 100m long on the SE side, extending down the hill, was enclosed with a curtain wall. This was a more modest affair than the inner curtain and very little of it remains but its layout is clear from the several old drawings which exist of the castle. It was divided into two lengthways by a wall against the NW side of which lay the stables. Both outer wall and crosswall had simple gateways facing SE. The inner part also had two more substantial gatehouses, the East Gate facing towards All Saints church and the West Gate facing towards the town. The latter, which is probably the Receiver's Tower mentioned in the 15th century, was 13th century in its lower parts and connected to the keep by a thick wall of that date. In a painting of the 1620s the two gatehouses are shown as lofty embattled towers. The curtain was embattled by the West Gate but the SE curtain and crosswall are shown as somewhat decayed, having lost their battlements. A passage about 15m long led to the West Gate from an irregular enclosure about 30m by 25m known as the barbican on the site of what is now called Castle Chain.

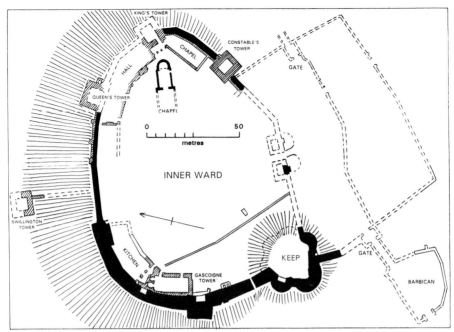

Plan of Pontefract Castle

The 12th century curtain wall of yellow magnesian limestone was of exceptional thickness, over 6m on the SW side, and about 4m on the NE side, and the early towers, all rectangular, seem to have formed no more than minor projections from it or just parts rising higher than the main wall-walk. On the SE side was a gateway flanked internally by two rectangular towers about 10m by 9m in size, an arrangement not likely to be earlier than the 1190s. Part of the southern tower still stands high, with an external buttress. Polygonal fronts with solid bases were added in the 14th century to extend the gatehouse beyond the curtain wall, and a portcullis groove remains in the extended passage, but since there is no evidence of these parts on the painting of the 1620s they may never have been completed above the bases. On the west side a wall extended down the slope to the Swillington Tower, a building about 13m wide, erected in 1400-05 by Henry IV and partly demolished in the 19th century for road widening. Henry also rebuilt the upper parts of the Constable's Tower, and probably also the King's Tower and the Queen's Tower around the NE end of the bailey, these works being executed with grey sandstone. Excavations have now cleared the lowest 4m of the Constable's Tower which was filled with rubble when the castle was demolished. It measured about 12m square and projected about 6m beyond the curtain wall. The basement, with a latrine at its junction on the north side with the curtain wall, is 12th or 13th century. Very little remains of the King's Tower (in front of which was an arcaded gallery) and only the infilled base of the Queen's Tower (with a latrine on the east side), which were also roughly 12m square and contained apartments for the people they were named after. A painting of c1625 suggests these three towers each had five storeys, and, although their height is exaggerated on the picture, they must have been over 18m high. Against the angled curtain between these two lay a 15th century hall block, its western gable being once the eastern end of an older block beyond which then became the "privy kitchen".

Between the King's Tower and Constable's Tower lay an Elizabethan chapel built to replace the 11th century collegiate chapel of St Cuthbert nearby. In the 12th century an east apse with pilaster buttresses was added to the original nave and chancel. Built against the SW curtain is a 15th century service suite consisting of a kitchen with four fireplaces against the outer wall and a bakehouse with a passage between the two backing onto the Treasurer's Tower. The bakehouse has two ovens backing onto the passage. Above it lay the steward's lodging. East of it is the base of the Gascoigne Tower. Next lay a postern through the wall in the foot of the motte ditch and beyond that is the probable position of the Piper's Tower. Cutting off the motte slope is a medieval garden wall including a stone seat. In front of this wall lies the entrance to a rock-cut cellar used to house prisoners during the Civil War and to store liquorice in the 18th century. It was originally reached by a still surviving spiral staircase and is thought to mark the site of the "old hall" mentioned in 1246 as needing repair. If so the motte ditch must have been filled by the early 13th century.

The stone keep (known as the Round Tower in old surveys) enclosed rather than stood upon the motte and had a unique plan. Beyond the angle of the curtain wall project three foils, the largest of them about 16m in diameter and still 7m high externally. On the evidence of Leland's description of the keep as being "cast into 6 roundells, 3 bigge and 3 smaull" it is thought that the destroyed inner part of the keep was in the form of three smaller foils. Overall the keep measured 30m across externally. The only surviving features are a latrine pit on the east, a rectangular space on the west and a stair zig-zagging down in long flights from the motte summit to a postern and well. Surveys of 1538 and 1643 indicate the keep had three storeys. The 1538 survey mentions six rooms on the lowest level, whilst the later survey says each level contained five rooms. The top level was then known as the "artelere" and presumably had cannon mounted upon it. This suggests there were stone vaults. The top level at least was added in the 1370s and old drawings show round bartizans projecting at the points where the foils interlocked. Facing the bailey at the foot of the motte is a medieval garden wall containing an original stone seat.

Kitchen at Pontefract

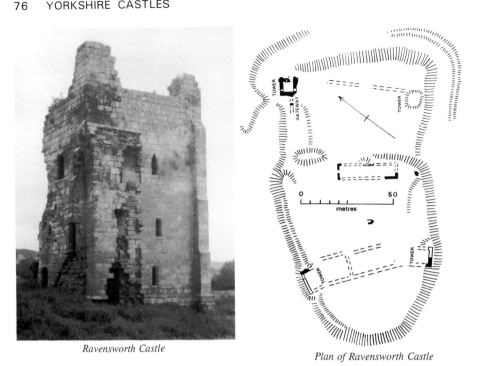

Ravensworth Castle

Plan of Ravensworth Castle

RAVENSWORTH CASTLE   NZ 142077   V

Only fragments remain of this large mansion, which was probably once surrounded by a broad wet moat. The best preserved part is the late 14th century 10m square tower at the north corner. A gateway with a portcullis groove adjoined the west side of it. There are stumps of walls and fallen fragments of rectangular towers at the west and south corners, whilst a platform may mark the site of an east tower. These would have marked the corners of a walled area 110m by 70m probably divided into two courts, with the innermost towards the SW. There are footings of a range between the west and south towers and the site platform extends here out beyond in a D-shape. East of this is a fragment of the Belfry Tower, upon which was an inscription, and in the middle of the site are ruins of a building about 33m by 9m.

Ravensworth was the seat of a family that from the mid 14th century became known as the Fitz-Hughs. King John is known to have visited them here in 1201. Henry Fitz-Hugh was licensed by Richard II to enclose 200 acres of parkland around the castle in 1391 and it is likely that he had recently rebuilt or extended the building. Henry, 6th Baron Fitz-Hugh founded a chantry within the castle chapel in 1467. On the death of George, 8th Baron Fitz-Hugh in 1512 the castle passed to Thomas Parr, Lord of Kendal. It reverted to Crown on the death of his son William, Lord Parr and Earl of Essex and Leland's description of the castle suggests most of it was already disused if not actually ruinous by the 1530s. Camden describes the castle as a ruin and there is a mention in 1608 of considerable pilfering of stone from the site by locals. What appears to be the chapel is shown on a late 18th century print by Grose, but a second print by him depicts little more of the ruins than survives today, except that the top of the Belfry Tower and parts of the south and west towers seem to have collapsed in the early 20th century.

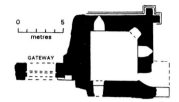

Ravensworth: gateway plan

RICCALL MANOR SE 616381

The former vicarage, remodelled by Street in 1869, is an impressive three storey brick tower house of c1500. At the NW corner is a projection only rising as high as the second storey, where it contains a room with a ribbed vault of brick. The SE corner has a square stair turret which turns octagonal higher up and ends with a corbelled-out chamber, capped by a pyramidal roof, and reached only by a ladder. It seems that originally there was a hall block to the south and possibly a second tower beyond it.

Riccall Manor

Richmond Castle

Richmond Castle

RICHMOND CASTLE   NZ 172008   E

After the death of Edwin, Earl of Mercia in 1071 his lands in Yorkshire were given to Alan the Red, son of the Count of Penthievre. By the time of his death in 1089 it is assumed that the curtain wall and Scolland's Hall had been built. He was succeeded in turn by his brothers Alan and Stephen, and then by the latter's son Alan, who married Bertha, heiress of the Duke of Brittany. Their son Conan, who built the tower keep, was thus not only Earl of Richmond but inherited the Dukedom of Brittany in 1164. Henry II managed to persuade Conan to resign the duchy and betroth his daughter to the king's third son Geoffrey. When Conan died in 1171 Henry II took possession of Richmond and held it until the young Constance and Geoffrey were finally married in 1181. The Pipe Rolls record work on the castle during that period costing over £100. It appears that the keep was then completed, the south wall of the main court was erected and the private garden to the east known as the Cock Pit was walled in stone. In 1174 William the Lion, King of Scotland was imprisoned in the castle after being captured at Alnwick. Geoffrey died in 1186 and Constance held the Honour of Richmond until her death in 1201, after which her third husband remained as a tenant until forfeited for rebellion against King John. Constance and Geoffrey had a son Arthur, who was captured and murdered by King John in 1203 as a dangerous rival with a better claim to the throne. For a while the Honour of Richmond was held by Ranulf de Blundeville, Earl of Chester, who had been Constance's second husband, until the union was annulled in 1197.

Peter de Braine, husband of the eldest of Constance's two daughters by her third marriage became Duke of Brittany and in 1218 obtained part of the Honour of Richmond. This estate was forfeited because the Duke sided with the King of France against Henry III. It was held by Peter of Savoy from 1240 until restored to the Duke of Brittany in 1266, his son John then being married to the king's daughter Beatrice. John in turn was forfeited for supporting the French in 1294 but reinstated in 1298. The domestic buildings show some signs of improvements during the time of John II, Duke of Brittany. After the death of Duke John III in 1341 Edward created his fourth son John of Gaunt Earl of Richmond. He surrendered the earldom on becoming King of Castile and Richmond was again returned to the Duke of Brittany. He was forfeited in 1381, and then again, finally, in 1384. Richard II then gave Richmond to his consort, Anne of Bohemia. Henry IV granted Richmond to Ralph Neville, Earl of Westmorland. From 1425 until 1435 the earldom was held by Henry VI's uncle, John, Duke of Bedford. Henry VI made his half-brother Edmund Tudor Earl of Richmond in 1453. He died in 1456 but left a posthumous son, who in 1485 became Henry VII. Before his accession he used the title Earl of Richmond although during the period of Yorkist ascendancy the castle was held in turn by Edward IV's brothers George, Duke of Clarence, and the Duke of Gloucester, eventually Richard III.

In 1525 Henry VIII created his illegitimate son Henry Fitzroy as Duke of Richmond, but the lad died in 1536, aged only 17. A survey carried out in 1538 recommended the construction of two new towers on the west side of the main court and a third on the north side of the Cock Pit, but this work was never executed. By then the walls were in serious decay. In 1623 James I revived the title for Ludovic Stuart. He died the same year and in 1641 Charles raised James Stuart, Earl of Lennox to the dukedom. The fifth duke of this creation died in 1672 and the castle was long held by the descendants of Charles Lennox, an illegitimate son of Charles II, who was created Duke of Richmond in 1675. The lower part of the keep had its robbed-out lower facing replaced and the battlements repaired in the 1760s, £350 being spent on the work. A barracks, now demolished, was erected on the west side of the court in the 19th century, and the keep was then used as a military store. The ruins were taken into State guardianship in 1910.

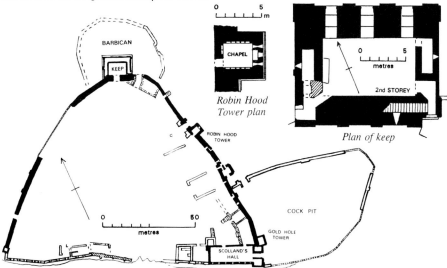

Robin Hood
Tower plan

Plan of keep

Plan of Richmond Castle

Richmond Castle

The castle consisted originally of just a single triangular court enclosed on the NW and east sides by a curtain wall up to 3.5m thick, whilst on the 130m long SW side a precipitous drop to the River Swale was originally considered enough protection. The NW side ends towards the river in a tall turret just over 4m square. The low loopholed walls facing the river east of here are late 12th century. Progressing towards the keep there is then an arch marking the site of a chapel with a postern below it, a section with two pilaster buttresses on the outside, and a 33m long section which is missing. The eastern side was more vulnerable to attack and was provided with three towers each about 6.5m square. The foundations on this side are inadequate and the centre section of the wall has bulged out, causing the collapse of the middle tower sometime after 1538, when it was described as decayed. The Robin Hood tower north of this bulge originally flanked a gateway which was blocked in the 12th century. The tower contains two barrel-vaulted rooms, the lower one a chapel of St Nicholas with wall arcading.

Beyond the well-preserved Gold Hole tower near the south end is another gateway leading straight into the basement of Scolland's Hall. This gateway is reached through a 12th century outer ward measuring 70m by 50m with its own gateway arch facing north near the main inner wall. This court, the Cock Pit, is now being restored to its medieval use as a garden. Most of its south wall is missing and also its eastern end where a tower is recorded in 1538. Scolland's Hall is named after one of the first earl's officials. It measures 23m by 9m internally contained a hall and chamber set over a basement with a row of seven loops looking out towards the river. The Gold Hole Tower contained latrines serving this block. The upper storey of the hall block probably had five windows each of two lights on each side. The south wall at this level was rebuilt in the late 12th century, when a set of steps up to the fine doorway was built against the NW corner and a block containing two rooms on each of two levels was added to the west. Beyond them, where the ground has subsided, once lay another tower. One window in the south side of the hall was replaced by a larger three-light window in the 14th century, and a window in the north wall replaced by a doorway. The original private chamber or solar seems to have been remodelled in the 13th century after a fire, the two light south window then being inserted. In the early 14th century a new solar was added to the north, beyond which was a chapel and another chamber, in line against the east curtain. The new solar has windows on either side of a fireplace in its each wall. The chapel was reached directly from the court by its own set of external steps and had a three-light west window. At the same time all the towers against the east curtain were given an additional third storey, that in the Gold Hole Tower having a fireplace and latrine.

The third and most important entrance to the 11th century castle lay through a gatehouse on the site of the present keep. Its inner archway still survives, and in the 19th century was unblocked to give access to the basement of the keep, in which is a 12th century octagonal central pier built over a well and supporting a 14th century rib-vault. A spiral stair leading up lies with the basement. The original gateway was superseded by a new archway pierced through the curtain wall immediately to the east. To give extra protection to both the keep and new gateway a polygonal court or barbican 50m by 30m was built out in front of them, but little remains of it. The new gateway was replaced in the 19th century when a barrack block was built behind this corner. Access to the upper levels of the keep is now by means of an external stair, over the roof of this building, and into the recessed SE corner of the keep. The keep measures 15m by 13.5m above the (refaced) stepped plinth on the three faces outside the court and stands 30m high. On the south side the mid-wall and corner clasping pilaster buttresses which elsewhere rise from the plinth start only at the level of the curtain wall-walk. The upper entrance admits to a hall with a central pier to support the next floor, three north facing windows, and small rooms in the thickness of the east and west walls. A straight stair in the south wall rises to the private chamber above, which is lighted by windows set above a second tier of mural chambers in the end walls. Another straight stair then runs up to the much restored battlements, which rise above the apex of the original keep.

In 1313 Edward II granted the townsfolk the right to raise taxes for walling in the town. An arch of one gateway and a narrow postern still remain with a few fragments. Originally there were two other gateways.

RIPLEY CASTLE   SE 283605   O

The Ingilbys have lived at Ripley since Sir Thomas married the heiress Edeline Thweng c1320. The outer gateway is 15th century but the tower house was built by Sir William Ingilby between 1548 and 1555, the dates being recorded by a frieze inside. An adjoining hall disappeared in a rebuilding of the rest of the castle in the 1780s by Sir John Ingilby, who managed to inherit despite being both illegitimate and a minor on his father's death. He borrowed heavily to fund the work and ended up fleeing abroad to escape his creditors, the house being left empty and unfinished from 1794 to 1804. The tower measures about 10m by 8m and is of three storeys which are connected by a spiral stair in the SW corner, which is strengthened by a diagonal buttress and rises up as a turret. The tower is of little military strength, having three-light windows at ground level, the room there now being the library.

The tower house at Ripley

Ripley Castle: the old tower appears on the left

RIPON MOTTE   SE 316711

Ailcy Hill is a large but very damaged motte. There is also a moated site with the possible base of a tower at North Lees (SE 302737).

ST JULIAN'S CASTLE   NZ 816009

The de Maulays are said to have had a stronghouse on this site. Traces of a large building formerly moated around were noted in 1750 and foundations and earthworks could still be traced until the late 19th century.

SANDAL CASTLE   SE 337181   F

The relationship between this motte and bailey site and another less than 2km away at Wakefield remains uncertain. The manor of Wakefield was granted by Henry I to William de Warenne, 2nd Earl of Surrey probably c1107, but the earthworks at Sandal may belong to a later period. William, 6th Earl of Surrey probably began rebuilding the castle at Sandal in stone in the 1230s, perhaps to make good damage during the recent civil war of Henry III's minority. In 1239 he was succeeded by his son John, then a minor. He must have continued the work during the 1250s and 60s. In 1268 he was heavily fined for an attack upon Lord Zouch, who was fatally wounded, but in 1272 he was received back into favour by the new king, Edward I and given the additional title of Earl of Sussex. Much of the building as it stood through the later medieval period probably existed by 1304, when his grandson John, another minor, succeeded him as 8th earl. The castle was seized by Earl Thomas of Lancaster in 1317 and held by him until his defeat and execution by Edward II in 1322. Later that year the king authorised repairs to Sandal Castle, which he had kept in his own hands, it only being returned to Earl John in 1326. When he died in 1347 the estate reverted to the Crown and was given by Edward III to his youngest son Edmund of Langley. From him descended the Dukes of York and the castle again became a Crown possession when Edward IV took the throne in 1461. He later granted Sandal to his brother, Richard, Duke of Gloucester. In 1484, during his brief reign, Richard rebuilt one of the towers of the keep. The castle decayed in the 16th century and was granted by Elizabeth I to Edward Carey in 1566. It was surrendered by Royalist garrison in October 1645 after being damaged by Parliamentary cannon-fire and was then dismantled.

Sandal, doorway in motte ditch

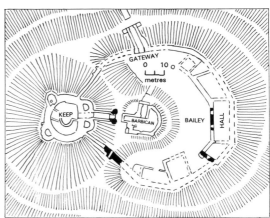

Plan of Sandal Castle

Inner barbican at Sandal

The castle consists of a motte lying on the west side of a D-shaped bailey 90m across, there being a deep ditch between and around both parts with a counterscarp bank. All that remained visible prior to excavation in 1964-73 were the south and west walls of the hall block on the east side of the bailey but a drawing of 1565 was evidence that the castle had once been a magnificent structure with a complex keep on the motte. The excavations revealed footings of various other chambers built against the bailey curtain wall, which was up to 3m thick. No traces of any towers remain, except for the gatehouse on the north side. Taking up much of the internal space was a barbican forming an additional defence for the access up to the keep. This barbican was a D-shaped court about 13m across reached on the north side by a drawbridge across its own ditch. From here a second drawbridge led over to a twin-turreted gateway into a another barbican formed by two parallel walls extending down the motte in front of the keep gatehouse. The keep was a shell keep with walls up to 3m thick above a plinth around a court 19m across which was mostly filled by lean-to internal buildings, leaving just a light-well 6m across. The thin wall around the light-well seems to have originally been the base of an early tower left incomplete. The outer wall was flanked by four round towers up to 8m in diameter, two of which were placed close together on the east side to flank the gateway. In 1484 a latrine was built beside the west tower and the north tower was rebuilt as a more thinly walled polygonal structure. Its basement contains a latrine and a well.

SAXTON MOTTE   SE 477367

This is a small damaged mound.

SCARBOROUGH CASTLE   TA 048892   E

The headland dominating the town was utilised by the Romans for a signal station guarding against seaborne raiders and from about 1000 a chapel stood on the site, but it does not appear that there was a castle here until 1138s, when William le Gros, Count of Aumale was created Earl of Yorkshire by King Stephen. He is said to have built a tower and wall before he was obliged to surrender the castle to Henry II in 1154. During the 1160s Henry II spent £650 on building a new keep and probably also the east curtain wall of the inner bailey. King John spent almost £2300 between 1202 and 1212 on work at the castle, firstly enclosing the west side of the inner bailey with a wall, and then building a screen wall for the west side of the outer bailey, whilst halls and chambers were erected in both baileys. In 1215 there was a garrison of ten knights, 72 sergeants, and 13 crossbowmen under the command of Geoffrey de Neville. A storm in 1237 unroofed several buildings and in the 1240s Henry III rebuilt sections of collapsed walling and erected the double drawbridge arrangement at the outer entrance. At the time of the peace arrangements made between Henry III and his barons in 1265 the castle was regarded as one of the strongest in the realm, alongside those of Bamburgh, Corfe, Dover and Nottingham. Edward I held court in the castle in 1275, and paid another visit in 1280, although in 1278 the outer drawbridge was too decayed for a cart to safely cross it. The castle was later used to incarcerate prisoners taken on his campaigns in Scotland.

Edward II repaired the castle and in April 1312 granted it to his unpopular favourite Piers Gaveston. After almost being captured by the infuriated barons at Newcastle, Gaveston took refuge in Scarborough Castle in May of that year. After a siege lasting a fortnight Gaveston agreed to surrender after being given a promise of safe conduct, but the Earl of Warwick ignored this and had him beheaded. The castle was subsequently in the custody of the Percy family, who erected a kitchen bakehouse and brewhouse in the inner bailey. However it was neglected for much of the time, and a section of wall collapsed in 1361. Richard III paid a short visit in 1484 to muster his fleet against Henry Tudor. In October 1536 the castle was besieged by the rebels during the Pilgrimage of Grace. The castle was badly damaged by cannonfire but Sir Ralph Eure and his garrison held out. In 1557 the castle was seized by Thomas Stafford, who was executed for treason at Tyburn after the castle had been quickly retaken by the earls of Shrewsbury and Westmorland. Subsequently the castle governor was ordered to live within the castle. The castle was garrisoned from the time of the Northern Rising of 1569 in favour of Queen Mary of Scots until the end of Elizabeth's reign in 1603. James I had no use for the castle and sold it to the Thompson family, who let out the headland as pasture.

In September 1642 Scarborough Castle was garrisoned for Parliament by Sir Hugh Cholmley. At the time when he changed sides early in 1643 he had a force of 600 infantry, 100 cavalry and 100 dragoons. Whilst he was away at York conferring with Charles I his cousin Captain Browne and a party of 40 seamen captured the castle in a surprise night attack. However Sir Hugh managed to persuade his cousin to return the castle to him. In January 1645 Scarborough was attacked by Lieutenant General Sir John Meldrum. After three weeks the defenders abandoned the town and retreated into the castle. Meldrum fell over a cliff edge whilst supervising the setting up of his artillery but was back in charge after six weeks, only to be killed later during an assault. The castle was bombarded with heavy artillery from the churchyard and from a rock outcrop to the west. After three day the upper part of the west wall of the keep collapsed. Somehow only two of the twenty men then on top of it fell to their deaths. The garrison still resisted all assaults until supplies ran out in July 1645, by which time only 25 of the defenders were said to be fit for duty.

The barbican at Scarborough

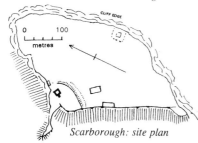

Scarborough: site plan

The keep at Scarborough

Parliament had the castle patched up and installed a garrison of 100 men with 60 gunners to man the batteries controlling the harbour. In July 1648 Colonel Boynton and his men, fed up with Parliament's failure to pay them, declared for the then captive King Charles. It was finally retaken in December and slighting was ordered but not executed. That the batteries covering the harbour were still needed was demonstrated in 1653, when a Dutch force under Admiral De Witt attacked a convoy of coal ships seeking refuge in the harbour. The castle was subsequently used as a prison, the Quaker George Fox being held in a room without heating and exposed to the rain in the Cockhyll Tower from April 1665 until September 1666.

After the 1745 rebellion the Mosdale Hall was reconstructed as a barracks which remained in use for about a century. This block was badly damaged by shellfire from the German battlecruisers Derflinger and Von de Tann in December 1914, some damage also being done to buildings in the town. The castle was taken into State guardianship for preservation as an ancient monument in 1920.

The headland is roughly lozenge-shaped, measuring 500m from north to south by 250m wide and has cliffs on all sides except to the SW, where there is a steep drop to a deep ditch. The inner bailey lies in the west corner, commanding the approach, which was through a 14th century outer barbican, over two drawbridges (now replaced by stone bridges) on either side of a mid 13th century inner barbican in the form of a gatehouse with round turrets with corbelled parapets perched on a pier in the middle of the great ditch, and then up to the now lost inner gatehouse immediately north of the keep. Just north of the site of this gatehouse is the 18th century Master Gunner's House. The 14th century outer barbican is a boot-shaped court 40m long with a gatehouse flanked by towers about 4m and 5m in diameter respectively. Two other smaller solid turrets flank the barbican wall further west.

Scarborough Castle

The elliptical inner bailey measured about 100m from north to south by 45m wide. Curving round the east side is a 12th century wall 1.6m thick, now reduced to its footings at the southern end, just north of which are traces of a gatehouse facing the 15m wide ditch. A hall block was later built inside this corner. Curving round the west side, but with a 15m gap between its broken off north end and the keep at the north end of the bailey, is King John's new outer wall 2.5m thick, with three solid round towers, two of them 8m in diameter and of shallow projection, whilst the third is smaller but projects more boldly. It bears a new viewing platform with metal steps.

Henry II's keep still stands 27m high and measures about 16m square over walls 3.6m thick at the level of the hall on the second storey. In the basement, which has just two loops facing NE, the walls are thicker internally and on the outside is a battered plinth from which rise clasping buttresses at the corners and in the middle of each side. The very outer corners each have a column rising the full height of the building. At the upper levels the floors were carried on internal offsets but the west wall probably had a constant thickness of 4.5m since it has in the middle a wide spiral staircase, on either side of which are pairs of shutes for latrines in chambers higher up. It would have been difficult to batter this thick but hollow wall with medieval siege engines, but in 1645 heavy cannon able to fire from long range destroyed most of it in a few days. On the SW side a straight stair leads up to the remains of a forebuilding with a pit prison below, and then a doorway led into the hall of the keep. From here a narrow stair led up to a chapel over the forebuilding. The hall has pairs of round-arched window embrasures facing NE and SE with a fireplace between the latter pair. The windows were of two round-headed lights like the better preserved ones in the king's private chambers on the level above. These third storey rooms were divided by a wall with a blind arcade set upon an arch spanning the hall and in turn providing a central support for the double roof above hidden below the wall-head. There was thus no fourth storey, the windows there being dummies. At the summit there were five turrets, one on each corner and one over the staircase.

The wall built by King John to enclose the rest of the headland extends 260m from the south corner of the inner bailey to where the Cockhyll Tower has vanished over the cliff at the south end. The wall is about 2m thick and 6m high, has rows of pilaster buttresses in places, contains two posterns and is flanked by five D-shaped towers containing two storeys of rooms furnished with arrow-loops, the largest tower being 9m in diameter. The polygonal second tower has been refaced in brick along with the section of wall south of it. This refacing is all that remains of the work of converting a chamber block against the wall here into a barracks. Only the two basement rooms now remain of this block, known as the Mosdale Hall. The medieval upper rooms were reached by external stairs at each end and had hearths in the middle of their floors. NE of this block are footings of an aisled hall, also early 13th century, with a kitchen beyond the service rooms at the NW end. The postern near the south end served as the access for a gun battery overlooking the harbour. First established in 1643, enlarged in 1652-7, and provided with an access from the postern in 1746, this battery remained in use until the 19th century. On the east side of the outer bailey are the confused remains of an early chapel built on the site of Roman signal tower and its surrounding court. The vaulted chamber there contains a well and was later converted into a water tank. The harbour was closed off by a wall before or during King John's reign. The town was then provided with a ditch and this was augmented by a stone wall in the 14th century. Leland mentions the town walls as having been repaired by Richard III. There are no remains of them.

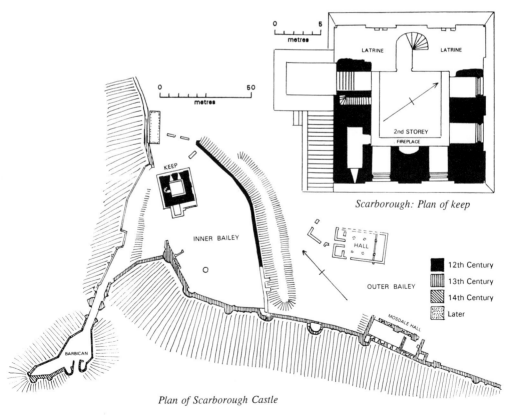

Scarborough: Plan of keep

Plan of Scarborough Castle

Mosdale Hall at Scarborough

SCARGILL CASTLE   NZ 398375

This castle was built in the 15th century by the Scargill family, who held the estate from the 12th century until it passed by marriage to the Tunstalls in 1530. It was probably allowed to decay after they acquired nearby Wycliffe in the mid 17th century. The castle consisted of a court about 28m by 21m with a hall 6.5m wide on the east and other ranges on the south and north. The northern part has vanished but the lower parts remain of the south end of the east range with one fireplace. The west side of the court was enclosed by a wall 1m thick from which projected a gatehouse 6.5m by 5.5m, now the principal survival. On the north side a spiral stair in a turret rises off to the entrance passage to two storeys of upper rooms.

SEAMER CASTLE   TA 013834

In a field west of the church is a ruined wall 1.5m thick containing a late medieval doorway and bearing signs of vaulting. The manor house here is referred to as a castle in 1547 and the remains suggest a possible tower house.

SELBY CASTLE

Nothing remains of the earthworks of a castle built to defend the abbey in 1143 and captured the same year.

Seamer Manor House

Keep stair, Scarborough

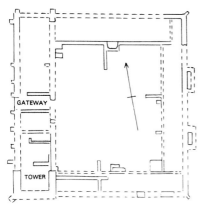

Plan of Sherburn Palace

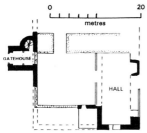

Plan of Scargill Castle

Scargill Castle

SHEFFIELD CASTLE   SK 358877

The Pipe Rolls of Henry II for 1184 refer to this castle as recently burnt. It then belonged to the Luvetot family. In 1270 Henry III granted a licence to Thomas Furnival for the site to be refortified. The large round tower which is recorded may have been built around that time. The castle was captured by Parliamentary troops in 1644 and then dismantled. The bases of two gatehouse towers are said to remain in the cellars under the market house.

SHERBURN PALACE   SE 543336

Within a moated platform measuring 64m by 55m foundations have been revealed of a manor house of the archbishops of York. Walls 1.2m thick enclosed a court about 36m square with ranges on all four sides. The 8.8m wide west range contained the principal rooms and there seems to have been a tower with slightly thicker walls at the SW corner. The other ranges were thinner and the internal walls were half-timbered on thin foundations. The chapel is thought to have been in the NE corner. There were several buttresses on the west side, diagonal buttresses at the NE and SE corners, and two wide latrine projections on the east. Most of these works, including the moat, seem to have been of about the time of the licence to crenellate granted by Richard II to Archbishop Alexander in 1383, prior to which there was a cluster of unfortified buildings on the site. The place was dismantled towards the end of Henry VIII's reign and then left unoccupied.

SHERIFF HUTTON CASTLE   SE 652662   V

South of the parish church at the east end of the village at SE 657662 is an overgrown ringwork 30m across and 3m high above its ditch, with traces of a bailey to the west. It is thought to have been built c1140 by Bertram de Bulmer and to have been captured for King Stephen by the Earl of Richmond. Geoffrey de Neville obtained the manor in 1176 by marriage to the Bulmer heiress. The towering fragments at the other end of the village are relics of a castle built by John Neville in the 1380s, a licence to crenellate being obtained from Richard II in 1382. He was currently also rebuilding his older castle at Raby in County Durham. His son Ralph, who succeeded in 1389 and was created Earl of Westmorland in 1397, is thought to have built the more thinly walled western corner tower. After the defeat and death of Richard Neville, Earl of Warwick (see Middleham) in 1471, Edward IV granted Sheriff Hutton to his own brother, Richard, Duke of Gloucester. In the 1490s the castle was occupied by Thomas Howard, Earl of Surrey as President of the Council of the North. Thomas Savage, the next President, was Archbishop of York and able to use his own seat at Cawood and by the time Henry VIII's illegitimate son Henry Fitz-Roy was sent north as the new President in 1525 the castle required over £320 worth of repairs. More work costing £196 was carried out in 1536, but after the Presidency of Thomas Howard, Duke of Norfolk, who was a prisoner in the Tower of London when Henry VIII died in 1547, the castle was mostly allowed to decay since his successors used their own houses or resided in the King's Manor beside the former abbey of St Mary at York. A survey in 1595 noted that some of the lead taken from the towers and buildings at Sheriff Hutton was alleged to have gone to the King's Manor at York. Part of the building was still in use as a prison for "recusant gentlewomen". In 1609 the then president, Lord Sheffield, asked for funds to repair Sheriff Hutton but nothing was forthcoming and in 1618 the ruinous building was granted to Thomas Lumsden, who removed what remained of the floors and roofs, although a 15th century range in the outer court long remained in use as a farmhouse. The site was granted to Sir Arthur Ingram in 1625 and was long held by his descendants.

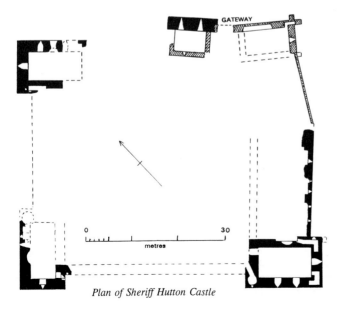

Plan of Sheriff Hutton Castle

Sheriff Hutton Castle   *Sheriff Hutton Castle*

Very little remains of the curtain walls except for a fragment on the SE side, but there are impressive fragments still standing over 25m high of the rectangular corner towers. The north, west and south towers each measured about 16m by 10m over walls 2.2m thick and had vaulted basements. They had latrines in their outer corners, some of them reached by long passages from rooms in the ranges between the towers, as at Bolton. The east corner and the NE wall do not seem to fit in with the regular pattern established by the other towers and their intervening ranges. There is a gateway here with the Neville arms in a panel above. The corner tower beside it seems to have been a more modest structure about 12m by 8m over walls 1.4m thick buttressed at the surviving outer corner. Beyond the gateway is a section of walling 3m thick with loops without the wide embrasures found elsewhere and a chamber backing onto it. This all suggests that an older structure remained standing on this part of the site in the 1380s and that the east tower was only built after part of it was removed in the early 15th century.

Not enough evidence remains to be sure of the layout of the main rooms. The SE range was probably 10m wide internally and seems to have contained a hall, but this may have been the lord's private hall, and the great hall may have been in the SW range. In either case the lord's bedchamber must have been in the south tower, by far the most complete part of the castle, the three upper storeys of which were reached by a spiral stair opening off the SW range. The north tower also had four storeys, whilst the west tower contained five. An establishment this size probably contained two sets of kitchens and service rooms, one perhaps in the SE range near the east tower and the other below the apartments in the NW range. The farm to the NE occupies the former outer court which contained offices, stables, and, according to Leland had three high towers, the central one being the outer gatehouse.

Sheriff Hutton Castle

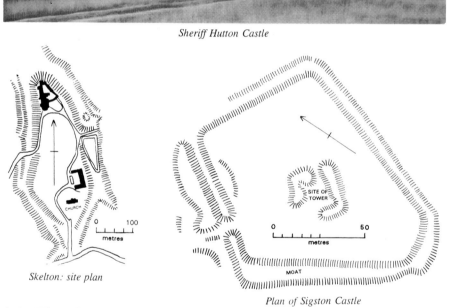

Skelton: site plan

Plan of Sigston Castle

SIGSTON CASTLE   SE 416952

Sigston belonged to the bishops of Durham and was granted by Bishop Pudsey in the late 12th century to his seneschal Philip Colville. However the surviving remains are perhaps more likely to date from 1336, when John de Sigston was licensed by Edward III to crenellate his house here. Soon afterwards it passed to the Place family, and then in the 15th century firstly to the Sywardebyes, and then the Pigots, being probably abandoned when the manor was divided in 1503. The 30m square mound in the middle of the site is probably the site of the house or tower. The surrounding enclosure measures 100m by 90m and has a 4m deep ditch, beyond which on the NW side is a higher outer bank. By the causeway of the moat on this side are traces of a probable gatehouse. Streams run past the SW and SE sides of the site.

SKELTON CASTLE   NZ 653193   V

A promontory nearly 500m long was provided with deep ditches widened out of the flanking valleys to enclose a castle at the north end and a village enclosure to the south. The parish church lies in the SE corner and near it lay the only access, with a ditch and gatehouse. The site may have been first fortified by Richard de Surdeval in the 1070s. It reverted to the Crown on his death in the 1090s and in 1119 was granted by Henry I to Robert de Brus. Adam de Brus, who died in 1196, and his son Peter are said to have refortified the castle in stone, when a rectangular keep is thought to have replaced the original motte. Peter sided with the barons against King John, who captured the castle in 1216.

In 1272 Skelton passed to the de Fauconberg family. When Thomas Fauconberg died in 1407 the castle, probably then ruinous, went to Ralph Neville's younger son William. He was created Earl of Kent two years before his death in 1463. The castle then passed to the Conyers family. After John Conyers' death in 1557 he left three daughters who are said to have each demolished their share, so bitter was the dispute between them over possession. What was left was described as "ruinous and of no value". The estate then passed to the Kempes only to be sold to the Trotters, one of whom is said to have inhabited part of the castle until it was sold by Lawson Trotter in 1732. Skelton then passed to John Hall who took the additional name of Stevenson. His grandson built much of what now stands in the 1790s, when a "magnificent tower" is said to have been demolished, but the structure incorporates two 14th century windows, probably in situ, of the original chapel, and there are also substantial 17th century parts, including several mullioned windows and a staircase.

SKIPSEA CASTLE   TA 162551   F

Footings of a stone gatehouse lie upon a high 11th century motte with a rampart beyond the ditch. A causeway across a former lake connected it to a long, narrow enclosure to the SW with a high rampart. This may have contained a village. During the brief rebellion of William de Forz, Count of Aumale in 1221 the castle was ordered to be destroyed. The site seems to have been long abandoned by the mid 14th century. See page 5.

Outer gatehouse at Skipton   *Inner gateway arch at Skipton*

The 16th century range at Skipton

SKIPTON CASTLE   SD 991520   O

In the late 11th century Skipton lay within an estate originally centred on Bolton which was granted by William II to Robert de Romille. His daughter and heiress married William Meschin, and the first mention of a castle at Skipton is in 1130, during their period of tenure. Their daughter Alice married William Fitz-Duncan, who became lord of Skipton in the 1150s. Cicely, their daughter married William le Gros, Earl of Aumale, the former owner of Scarborough Castle. This couple's grandson, William le Fortibus, heir of the daughter Hawise, became Earl of Albemarle. It was his son William, 2nd Earl of Albermarle, lord of Skipton from 1194 until 1241, who rebuilt the castle in stone. It eventually passed to yet another heiress, Aveline de Forz, on whose death in 1274 Skipton reverted to the Crown.

Throughout Edward I's reign Skipton was retained as a royal castle but on his accession in 1307 Edward II granted it to his favourite Piers Gaveston. In 1310, however Edward arranged for the estate to be transferred to Robert de Clifford. After he was killed in the English defeat at Bannockburn in 1314 the castle was said to be "much in need of repair". In 1318 the Scots sacked the town but the castle seems to have not been affected. Robert's son Roger was forfeited for his part in the rebellion of Thomas of Lancaster but Edward III returned the estate (or Honour) of Skipton to Robert de Clifford in 1330. The chapel was built around that time, and a new wall to enclose an extensive outer bailey.

John, 9th Lord Clifford, was a staunch Lancastrian who got the nickname "The Butcher" from having cut off the head of Richard Duke of York, who had been killed in the battle of Wakefield in 1460, to set the gruesome relic up over one of the gates of York city. This was done in revenge for the death of Thomas, 8th Lord Clifford when York and his followers stormed St Albans in 1455. After Lord Clifford was in turn killed in the battle of Towton in 1461 the new king, Edward IV, confiscated the estate, which was subsequently held in turn by Sir William Stanley and Richard, Duke of Gloucester. Henry, 10th Lord Clifford came out of hiding as a shepherd in Cumberland to reclaim Skipton after Henry VII's accession in 1485. He provided new apartments in the inner ward. His son Henry was created Earl of Cumberland by Henry VIII. The castle was besieged and nearly captured by the rebels during the Pilgrimage of Grace of 1536. The rebel leader, Robert Aske, was related to the Cliffords and many of the earl's tenants joined the rebellion. The long gallery is said to have been built in a single season to be ready in time for the marriage that year of Henry, the future 2nd Earl, with Henry VIII's niece Lady Eleanor Brandon.

The Conduit Court at Skipton

Over the inner ward gateway is an inscription recording "This Skipton Castle was repayred by the Lady Anne Clifford, Covntesse Dowager of Pembroke, Dorsett, and Montgomery, Baroness Clifford, Westmorland, and Veseie, Lady of the Honor of Skipton in Craven, and High Sheriffesse by inheritance of the covntie of Westmorland, in the years 1657 and 1658, after this maine part of itt had layne rvinovs ever since Decemner 1648, and the Janvary followinge, when itt was then pvlld downe and demolisht, allmost to the fovndacion, by the command of Parliament, then sitting at Westminster, becavse it had been a garrison in the then civill warres in England". Lady Anne, last of the Cliffords at Skipton, was the daughter of George, 3rd of Cumberland and inherited Skipton from her uncle, Francis in 1643. She had already outlived several notable husbands and died in 1676, aged 86. Cromwell allowed her to restore the castle as a residence on condition that the roofs were not strong enough to mount cannon, the castle having only been surrendered by Sir John Mallory in December 1645 after a siege of several months by Parliamentary forces. The slighting had been ordered after a short-lived reoccupation of the castle by a party of Royalists in 1648. After Lady Anne's death Skipton passed to the 4th Earl of Thanet. The last of this line was the 11th Earl, who died in 1849, when the castle passed to Sir Richard Tufton. The long gallery remains in use as a private residence. The inner ward rooms remain roofed and floored but contain no furnishings, serving purely as an ancient monument open to the public.

The hall at Skipton

The castle lies on ground rising to a sheer cliff to the Eller Beck on the north side. In its original form with timber buildings there was probably a motte on the site of the inner ward with a bailey platform west of it, where the stables and chapel now lie. The town now lies to the south, further down the hill, but in the 12th century perhaps occupied the rest of the existing outer ward and the space to the south of it, traces of an early ditch and rampart having been found in excavations. The parish church, now a mostly 14th and 15th century building, but a 12th century foundation, lies less than 20m beyond the outer ward wall and would have compromised its defence. This outer ward measures 200m long from east to west by 75m wide. It may have only had a palisade during the medieval period. The existing thin wall, with the one survivor of its five or six bastions and the outer gatehouse probably date from after when the 10th Lord Clifford was restored to his estates in 1485. The bastion and the gatehouse towers have plinths with mouldings not likely to be earlier than the 15th or early 16th century and the gatehouse arch is of early Tudor type. The gatehouse main block contains chambers on either side of the passageway. It measures about 16m square and has four thinly walled round corner towers about 7.5m in diameter. The towers probably once rose above the main block but when the upper parts were rebuilt c1660 the towers were embattled at probably a lower level than originally and the central part of the main block now rises above them with pierced in its parapet the Clifford motto "Desormais (henceforth!)".

The chapel of St John remains roofed but otherwise open to the elements, the side windows lacking mullions, tracery or glass, although the east window has been restored since being discovered when an adjoining building was demolished. The castle had a chaplain (and presumably a chapel) by Henry II's reign but the existing building is early 14th century. It was used for family weddings and baptisms as late as the 1630s but soon afterwards was converted into a stable, a floor being inserted to accommodate the grooms over the horses.

Within its thick outer wall the D-shaped inner ward measures only 35m by 24m and is mostly filled with two storeys of rooms, leaving an open court just 10m wide by 15m on its longest northern side. It is known as the Conduit Court from the cistern below it. This cistern supplemented a water supply piped in from outside. In the middle of the court is a yew tree with panelled seating around the trunk. The straight northern side of the inner ward overlooks the drop to the beck. Closely grouped around the rest of the ward, i.e. not more than 8 or 9m apart, are five drum towers. The three ranged around the east and south sides are massive structures up to 10.5m in diameter over walls up to 2.9m thick above broadly battered plinths. These towers contain loops with cross-shaped arrow slits and probably date from c1220-40. It is likely that they originally had three storeys with the topmost rising above the main walls and roofs. As they are at present everything above the moulding about half way up on the exterior is rebuilding work of the 1650s with much thinner walling than below. Two of these three towers thus now have a medieval lower storey and a top storey which is partly medieval and partly restoration. The third, facing south towards the outer gate, and consequently known as the Watch Tower, rises slightly higher (to about 17m) and has two upper storeys, the junction of old and new work being clearly visible in the middle room.

The two western towers are earlier, probably dating from c1200, smaller at about 9m in diameter, and better preserved, although they may have lost an original third storey in the slighting. These towers flank the gateway passage 2.4m wide, which retains a portcullis groove and a round inner arch of Norman type rebated for doors. What is now a vaulted dungeon reached by steps down from the entrance passage to the northern tower seems to have originally been the open pit of a counterbalanced drawbridge. The two storey porch in front of the gateway bears the Lady Anne's inscription below the bay window over the outer doorway, which faces south. Although now mostly of her period, this porch probably goes back to the 1490s, a more likely period for the pit to have been made into a dungeon than the 1650s.

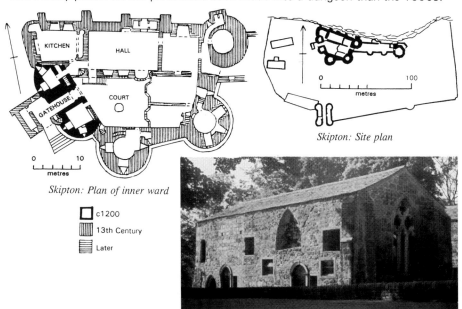

KITCHEN

HALL

GATEHOUSE

COURT

0   10
metres

Skipton: Plan of inner ward

0   100
metres

Skipton: Site plan

◻ c1200

▥ 13th Century

▤ Later

Chapel at Skipton

Skipton Castle

Skipton Castle

The domestic buildings around the Conduit Court are mostly of c1490-1520, with improvements of the late 16th century and remodelling of the 1650s. Before the 1490s the domestic buildings were perhaps mostly timber framed, or possibly even lay in the outer ward. Steps on the north side of the Conduit Court lead up to the service end of the hall. This room measures about 15m by 7m and is lighted by three windows towards the court, the easternmost being an oriel lighting the dais or platform for the lord's table. Curiously, there are no north facing windows, the only feature on that side being a fireplace. One of a pair of doorways with ogival hoodmoulds topped by fleur-de-lis leads through a service room to the kitchen. This room has northern facing windows at a high level, fireplaces at the east and west ends, and access to a latrine opening out over the cliff-face.

Off the hall east end is a doorway to the withdrawing room with a wide north facing window. South of here are the lord's private living room and his bedroom, each with bay windows facing west towards the court. A passage from the living room leads to the muniment room in the SE tower and stairs lead down to the wine and beer cellars under the withdrawing room. Another passage leads out to the mid 16th century range containing a long gallery on its upper floor. This range extends out to a three storey octagonal tower about 12m in diameter. Although its features look 16th century, this tower has thick walls and is probably an older structure. In the 1680s the Earls of Thanet remodelled the gallery into apartments (which are still occupied) and a room under the lord's living room was then adapted as a kitchen. At this level there is a doorway between the two bay windows facing the Conduit Court. Over the doorway are the arms (probably carved in the 16th century) of the 9th Lord Clifford, who was killed in 1461. The arms over the doorway leading into the Watch Tower are those of Margaret Bromflete, mother of the 10th Lord Clifford.

SKIRPENBECK MOAT   SE 750573

A stream has been used to fill a series of moats including one central island platform 4m high with a causeway approach on the east facing the church. Roger de Chauncey is recorded as holding a manor with a garden and two mills here in Edward I's reign. At SE 737580 is a small motte on the edge of a drop to the river .

SLINGSBY CASTLE   SE 696749   V

The "capital messuage" here in 1302 was probably built about a century earlier by the Wyvilles. In 1343 Ralph de Hastings purchased the house from William Wyville and in 1344 he obtained from Edward III a licence to crenellate it. Another licence, allowing crenellations and machicolations, was obtained from Edward IV by William Lord Hastings in 1474. He was executed shortly after Richard III seized the throne in 1483. Sir Charles Cavendish purchased the ruined house in 1595 and in 1603 began replacing it by a new mansion. His son William was created Duke of Newcastle by Charles II in 1664. There was a fresh grant of this title by William III in 1694 to John Holles, Earl of Clare, who inherited Slingsby about that time. It passed by marriage in 1717 to Edward Harley, later went to the Duke of Buckingham, and then in 1751 was sold to the Earl of Carlisle. The 17th century mansion is now very ruinous and overgrown. It incorporates a medieval wall up to 2m thick on its south side and lies within a platform surrounded by a ditch 20m deep which may have contained water and is now very overgrown on the north and west sides. The platform is revetted in stone on the east side, where there are gardens in the ditch.

Skipton Castle

Snape Castle

Snape Castle

SNAPE CASTLE   SE 262844   V

This building is thought to have been erected by George Neville, 1st Lord Latimer, who died in 1469. It lies on or near the site of a house erected in 1250 by Ralph Fitz-Ranulph. Although embattled, and presumably once moated, it was not seriously fortified and on old prints it is labelled as Snape Hall. Richard III's wife Anne Neville spent her later years at Snape with Richard's mother Cecily, and Katherine Parr, later Henry VIII's sixth and last wife, lived at Snape as the bride of Lord Latimer until his death in 1542. Upon the death of John Neville, 4th Lord Latimer it passed to Thomas Cecil, 2nd Lord Burghley, who was married to the heiress Dorothy. The house originally formed four ranges around a court and measured overall about 54m by 42m. In the mid 16th century the three storey east half of the south range was remodelled and the NE and SE corner towers were added, whilst in the 1580s Thomas Cecil rebuilt the two storey west end of the south range and the two western towers. However Thomas and Dorothy rarely visited Snape since their main residence was Burghley House in Huntingdonshire, more convenient for attendance at court.

By the 18th century the Cecils had no further use for their decayed house at Snape, which was sold in 1798 to the Milbanks, who held the neighbouring estate of Thorpe Perrow. The south range, which was divided by the Millbanks into two separate dwellings, remains inhabited and has mostly windows with later wooden frames except for one mullion-and-transom window of three lights high up in the east part. Inside are a late 16th century panelled plaster ceiling with the arms of the Cecils and Nevilles and further west a staircase and some panelling of the 17th century. The southern towers are of four storeys and contain several blocked windows. The SE tower has a straight joint between the original slim 15th century part (the parapet of which is not crenellated) and the 16th century extension. Adjoining it is the chapel, which although much restored has two 15th century windows of three lights facing south. Little of the east range stands above the series of vaulted cellars each with 15th century doorways facing the court. A higher fragment adjoins the NE tower, which is set back 9m from the east range outer face so that it only flanks the north side. It stands in a ruinous state to four storeys, with several mullion and transom windows. West of it are several cellars remaining of the eastern part of the north range. The NW tower also stands four storeys high, again in a very ruinous condition.

Snape Castle

Spofforth Castle

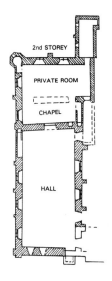

2nd STOREY

PRIVATE ROOM

CHAPEL

HALL

13th Century

14th Century
15th Century
Later & Modern

0   15
metres

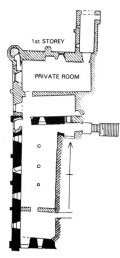

1st STOREY

PRIVATE ROOM

Spofforth: plans
See pages 13 & 101

SPOFFORTH CASTLE   SE 361511   F

William de Percy was given considerable estates in Yorkshire by William I and is thought to have had his main seat at Spofforth. In the late 13th century the male line of this family died out but Josceline de Louvain, Duke of Brabant agreed to assume the Percy surname upon his marriage to the heiress Agnes. In 1308 their son Henry obtained a licence from Edward II to embattle his house at Spofforth. Soon afterwards, however, he purchased Alnwick in Northumberland from Anthony Bek, Bishop of Durham, and he then remodelled the castle there as his principal seat, although he also had several other seats, notably Warkworth (also in Northumberland), so the importance of the house at Spofforth gradually declined.

In 1377 Henry, 4th Baron Percy of Alnwick was created Earl of Northumberland. He was killed fighting against Henry IV at the battle of Bramham Moor and his son Henry (known as Hotspur, and said to have been born at Spofforth) was killed in the battle of Shrewsbury in 1403. Their Yorkshire estates were then given by Henry IV to the Sheriff or Yorkshire, Sir Thomas Rokeby. The Percies later regained their estates but lost them again after the Yorkist victory at the battle of Towton in 1461, in which the 3rd earl, his brother Richard, and Sir William Plumpton, steward of Spofforth, were all killed. The estate was then held by the Earl of Warwick, who had burnt the castle shortly after the battle, until the Percies regained it in 1470. The house at Spofforth was renovated early in Queen Elizabeth's reign, but after the death of Sampson Ingleby, steward of the estate, c1604 the house was probably allowed to decay. It is said to have been wrecked in the Civil War.

The castle has been built upon and against a low rocky outcrop west of the village. Nothing remains of any curtain walls, gatehouse or ancillary buildings but on the west side of the site is a ruined 15th century hall 25m long by 12m wide of four bays with two-light windows. The south wall contains 14th century work, whilst below is an early 13th century cellar, narrower than the hall since it was built against the outcrop. In the 14th century the cellar was rib-vaulted with a row of three piers. The cellar is reached by a flight of steps leading down to the NE corner, and the hall entrance lay above it. The crosswall dividing off the south end of the lower level is 14th century. A projecting latrine of that period at the SE corner was removed when a wing was added beyond in the 16th century. North of the hall is a block assumed to date from about the time of the 1308 licence to crenellate. It contained a solar with two light windows set over what was perhaps an office, since it has a fireplace in the north wall. A spiral stair in a polygonal NW turret connected the two levels, both of which had latrines in a thinly walled projection to the NE. There are rooms between these chambers and the hall and its undercroft, the uppermost being probably a chapel originally, although later converted to a chamber with a latrine in its east wall.

Gatehouse at Steeton Hall

Temple Hirst

STEETON HALL   SE 483314

Although partly Tudor and Victorian, the house contains several medieval windows, including some sizeable ones close to the ground. A rib-vaulted room has been claimed as the chapel which was licensed in 1342. In front is a small detached gatehouse dated on heraldic evidence to c1360. It has an upper room with a corbelled out fireplace breast reached by an external stair, and a corbelled parapet at the summit. The curtain wall has gone but evidence of a moat around a large enclosure still survives.

SWINE: CASTLE HILL   TA 125343

This castle is said to have been built by Sir John Saher in the late 12th century. In 1353 John de Sutton was fined for crenellating his castle here (it lies in the parish of Sutton and was once called Bransholm) without royal permission. No stonework remains but brick foundations have been revealed and there is a much mutilated oval platform 100m long by 70m wide surrounded with a ditch with a counterscarp bank on the east and north sides.

TADCASTER CASTLE   SE 484436

Of a castle of the Percies here on the west bank of the Wharfe there remain a much mutilated but formerly large and lofty motte and the northern rampart of the bailey to the west. Leland describes the motte as a "mighty great hill". Stonework on the motte may relate to its later use as a pleasure garden.

TEMPLE HIRST   SE 592272

This a late medieval brick house with an embattled octagonal stair turret at one corner. Footings of a second turret have been exposed. Originally there were several turrets and a moat, and the house was described as a castle in the 16th century. The Norman doorway with a keeled roll-moulding is a relic of the preceptory of the Knights Templar here. After their suppression in 1310 it passed to the Darcy family.

THIRSK: CASTLE GARTH   SE 484436

This was one of the castles of Robert de Mowbray, Earl of Northumberland, which fell to the Crown in 1095 after his rebellion. Henry I granted the manor to Nigel d'Aubigny, who married one of the Mowbrays, and their son Roger, who adopted the de Mowbray surname, probably refortified the site in the 1140s. After the rebellion of 1174 Henry II seized the castle and demolished it in 1176. There are traces of the bailey but little remains of the motte, which lay on the north side of Castlegate.

THORNE: PEEL HILL   SE 689133

North of the church is a motte rising 6.5m to a summit 16m across on which footings of a round or octagonal stone keep are said to have once been visible. The site is said to have once been an island in a swamp. It is thought to have been used by the Warennes when hunting in Hatfield Chase. See page 4.

THORNHILL HALL   SE 256189

This is an irregularly shaped moated platform, 60m wide at the south end, where the corners are more or less right-angled. Along the 70m long east side and the NW side are traces of a retaining wall about 1.4m thick. These two sides meet at a sharp angle from which projected a bastion about 9m wide. The NW wall has pilaster buttresses. Excavations from 1964 to 1972 revealed footings of a rectangular gatehouse on the east and parts of a hall standing isolated in the middle of the platform. Of this a chimney breast remains standing, together with the south wall of a domestic east wing with two-light windows of mid 15th century type. Thornhill belonged to the Savile and was destroyed after a siege in the Civil War, although the curtain wall seems to have been dismantled about two generations earlier than that.

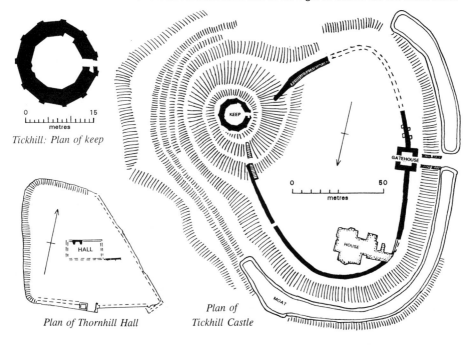

0 15
metres

Tickhill: Plan of keep

Plan of Thornhill Hall

Plan of Tickhill Castle

KEEP

GATEHOUSE

HOUSE

0 50
metres

MOAT

HALL

The motte at Tickhill

TICKHILL CASTLE   SK 594928

Roger de Busli is described as having a castle here (known as Blyth) in Domesday Book in 1086. His heir Roger was probably a minor in 1102 when Robert de Bellesme held the castle during his rebellion in support of Robert Curthose until it was besieged and captured by Robert Bloet, Bishop of Lincoln. The bailey curtain wall and the square gatehouse date from that period. Only footings remain of an eleven-sided tower keep built by Henry II on the motte summit, expenditure upon it being recorded in 1178-9. Hugh de Puiset, Bishop of Durham, besieged the rebellious Prince John's garrison in the castle in 1194, which only surrendered when the imprisoned Richard I returned to England and John was brought to obedience. During his reign John spent over £300 on building a barbican, a kitchen, a stable, a granary and work on the moat. Given by Henry III to Prince Edward in 1254, and then handed over to the prince's wife Eleanor, the castle was captured after a siege in 1264. Sir William de Anne successfully held out against a three week siege by the rebel barons in 1322. It then belonged to Edward II's consort Queen Isabella and was later granted to Edward III's consort Queen Philippa. It became part of the Duchy of Lancaster, merged with the Crown since 1399, when it was given to John of Gaunt in 1372 as part of an exchange of lands. The barbican in front of the gatehouse is probably 15th century, which suggests some maintenance during that period, although no royal visits are recorded. A survey of 1538 described the castle as decayed but it was garrisoned by Royalists in the Civil War until besieged and captured after their defeat at Naseby in 1644. Soon afterwards the keep and a 50m long section of the bailey curtain wall on the south side were destroyed, the parapets knocked off the rest of the wall and gatehouse and part of the south moat filled in.

The 6m high curtain wall encloses an oval bailey 115m by 85m and stands above a steep (and much overgrown) bank down to a water-filled moat 9m wide. Apart from the long breach on the south a short section is missing behind the 19th century house on the north side of the bailey. It is likely that the original domestic buildings lay there, since a plain Norman arch is incorporated in the house. The plain postern doorway on the NE side of the bailey may be original. The gatehouse on the west side measures about 11m square over walls 2.3m thick. The outer side is decorated with diapered triangular panels with crude figures. The upper storey has a fireplace and a five-light window of the late 16th century. The 23m high motte on the east side of the bailey is exceptionally large. Beyond its outer ditch, which is now dry, is a counterscarp bank. The motte summit, 24m across, is reached by a spiral path. The keep measured 17.4m in diameter over walls 3.2m thick with pilaster buttresses on the outer corners. The basement seems to have had a fireplace and a well and was entered direct from outside through a doorway closed by a portcullis. See p106.

Upsall Castle

Gateway at Tickhill

Oriel at West Tanfield

TOPCLIFFE CASTLE   SE 410750

The original seat of the Percies at Topcliffe was the Maiden Bower, a C-shaped bailey platform 80m by 70m with a rampart rising 2.5m above a ditch 1m deep and having a motte on the east, towards the Cod Brook. The motte rises 13m above the brook but only 3m above the bailey, and there is a 3m deep ditch between the two. This site may be that fortified by Geoffrey Plantagenet, Bishop of Lincoln, in 1174. By the 14th century a new house had been built within the earthwork known as the Manor Hills just 50m to the NE. This had an inner enclosure about the same size as the castle bailey lying on the SW side of an outer court 170m square with a rampart rising up to 5m above a ditch 1m deep. The entrance faces NW and the gaps facing NE and SE are modern. Despite these defences a local mob managed to break in and murder the 4th Earl of Northumberland in 1489.

UPSALL CASTLE   SE 455870

Geoffrey le Scope is said to have begun building a castle here soon after obtaining the manor from the de Upsall family. On the death of a later Geoffrey le Scrope in 1517 the castle passed by marriage to Sir James Strangeways. It changed hands several times and in 1578 went to Sir John Constable. His descendants, later viscounts Dunbar, held the castle until it was sold 1768, although the building itself is thought to have been wrecked during the Civil War. The remains lie in the garden of a mansion of 1876. It had a court about 58m by 53m with square towers at three corners and an octagonal tower at the NW corner. Part of this tower stands 4m high and the lower parts of the 40m long south and west curtains also remain, together with the 3m high base of the SE tower, which is a square of 18m. In the early 19th century the north curtain still stood 5m high and had a gateway facing towards the former outer ward.

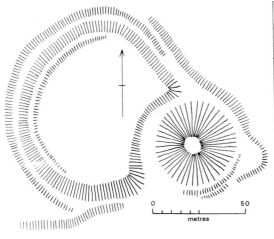

The Maiden Bower at Topcliffe

West Tanfield: old print

WAKEFIELD CASTLE   SE 326197   F

In a public park high above the River Calder is the earthwork once known as Low Hill. It consists of a worn down motte rising about 7m above a bailey platform, to the NE, with traces of a possible outer bailey beyond. The motte has a ditch on the NW. There is a mention of the constable of this castle in the 1170s, along with those of Tickhill and Conisborough. The site was later abandoned in favour of Sandal.

WALBURN HALL   SE 142959

This building has three ranges around a court with a low curtain wall with a wall-walk and embattled parapet on the fourth, facing the public road. The range opposite the curtain seems to be early 16th century, with an oriel of that period. The east range with mullion-and-transom windows is later 16th century. The other range, now ruinous, may have contained the chapel.

Walburn Hall

WEST TANFIELD CASTLE   SE 268787   V

In 1314 John Marmion obtained a licence from Edward II to crenellate his house "called L'Ermitage in his wood at Tanfield". A spur in a bend of the River Ure at SE 237774 is cut off by a ditch and bank to make a very large court on the north side of which are two enclosures with ramparts and ditches. The inner one, to the north, beyond which is a steep drop, has buried foundations of a house and chapel.

John Marmion's widow Matilda obtained a licence in 1348 for the crenellation of her manor house at "Westcanfield" but the surviving gatehouse perched above the north bank of the River Ure immediately SW of the church is more likely to have been built in the 15th century by the Fitz-Hugh family. It measures 10.3m by 9.5m and contains a passage 3m wide flanked on the south side by a guard room. A spiral stair leads to two upper rooms, the lower one having a fine oriel window facing east, whilst the upper one was a bedroom with a latrine corbelled out on the south side. Any courtyard attached to this gatehouse would have been of little defensive value since it would have been overlooked by the 15th century west tower of the church. The estate passed by marriage to Sir John Grey, whose son John assumed the surname Marmion. It passed to the Fitz-Hughs on the latter's death in 1385. From them it passed c1512 to the Parrs. Leland describes only a "hall of squared stone" at Tanfield apart from the "fair towered gatehouse". The castle reverted to the Crown on the death of William Parr, Marquis of Northampton in 1571. Elizabeth I granted it to William Cecil, Lord Burghley. His son, Thomas, Duke of Exeter is said to have demolished the hall block to provide materials for alterations to Snape Castle. The site passed to the Bruces, Earls of Elgin and Aylesbury in 1622, and their descendants held it until 1886.

Gatehouse at West Tanfield

Whorlton: interior of gatehouse

WHELDRAKE CASTLE

Under the name Coldric this castle is mentioned in 1149 when it was captured by King Stephen from a rebel garrison who were using it as a base for raids on York. The king then handed the castle over to the townsfolk for them to dismantle it, and presumably make use of the timber. In 1200 King John permitted Richard Malebisse to build a new castle on or near the same site. This verbal permission was revoked at the request of the citizens of York, who were threatened by it.

WHITWOOD MOTTE   SE 399349

Beside the River Calder is a 6m high motte with slight traces of a ditch.

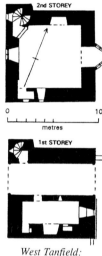

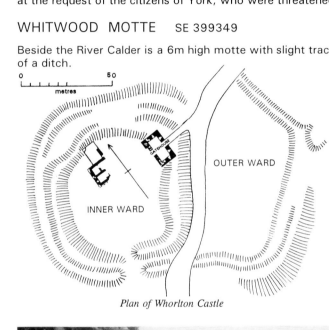

Plan of Whorlton Castle

West Tanfield:
Plans of gatehouse

Gatehouse at Whorlton

WHORLTON CASTLE   NZ 481025   F

The earthworks here were probably the work of the de Meynells in the late 11th century but this stronghold is first recorded in 1216 as the "castle of Potto". It was ruinous when Nicholas de Meynell died in 1342. The gatehouse and perhaps also the tower house are thought to have been built by Sir John Darcy, who obtained the manor by marriage in 1348. On the death of Sir Philip Darcy in 1418 the castle passed via an heiress to Sir James Strangways. After a dispute over possession the Crown took possession and in 1544 Henry VIII granted it to Matthew Stuart, Earl of Lennox. His grandson was James VI of Scotland, who became James I of England in 1603. he granted it to Edward Bruce, Lord Kinloss. The castle must have been let to tenants during this period and was probably ruinous, and from the 17th century until the late 18th century there was a house against the west end of the gatehouse.

The gatehouse lies on the east side of an inner ward 60m by 47m with a ditch and an outer bank on all sides, except towards where there was an outer ward 80m by 45m on the SE side. Further earthworks to the east may be relics of the lost village or fishponds. The gatehouse is 9m high and measures 17.6m by 10m above a plinth, the walls being 1.7m thick towards the inner ward and 2.2m thick on the other sides. The lowest level had a central passage with inner and outer portcullises. Over the outer entrance are shields with the arms of the Meynells, Darcys and Greystokes. Timber partitions separated the passage from a pair of rooms each with a latrine and one loop in each of the three outer walls. Above these rooms were others with mullion-and-transom windows. A spiral stair in a projection at the north end of the west wall and entered only from the outside led up to a more thinly walled upper storey with more mullion-and-transom windows. This seems to have been a court-room since it had several doorways into it leading off a passage in the west wall leading from the staircase. At the end of the passage a stair led up to the battlements. In the north corner of the inner ward are three cellars which are all that remain of the tower house. It stood about 7m high in 1725 but was mostly demolished in 1876 to provide stone for a new church at Swainby. See p109.

Tower house remains at Whorlton

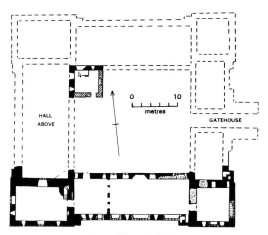

Plan of Wressle Castle

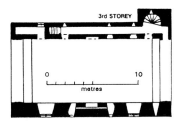

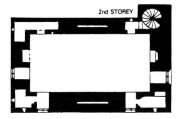

Shields at Whorlton

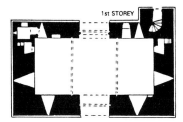

Whorlton: plans of gatehouse

WILTON CASTLE NZ 581196

A castellated building designed by Sir Robert Smirke for Sir John Lowther lies on or near the site of a tower demolished c1807 which is assumed to have been a relic of the manor house Ralph de Bulmer was licensed to crenellate by Edward III in 1330. The estate was confiscated from the Bulmers after the Pilgrimage of Grace and later passed to the Cornwallis family. The decayed castle was sold to Sir Stephen Fox c1700, and then again to Katherine Fowler in 1748.

WILTON CASTLE SE 863829 V

East of the church is a platform 80m by 65m with a ditch up to 14m wide and 3m deep with an outer bank on the south side and an outer enclosure beyond. The slight traces of a curtain wall are likely be a relic of what was built in accordance with a licence to crenellate granted by Edward III to John de Heslerton in 1335. He or his father acquired the manor in 1309, but the site was occupied long before that as excavation revealed traces of 12th century occupation. In 1375 Wilton passed to John de Hotham. Leland describes it as a manor place with a tower belonging to one of the Cholmley family who had inherited it from one of the Hastings family, but it later reverted to the Hothams. It is first referred to as a castle in the early 17th century and seems to have been destroyed during the Civil War, probably after the execution of John Hotham in 1645 after he deserted to the Royalists.

WRESSLE CASTLE   SE 707316

This splendid palace was probably erected in the 1390s by Thomas Percy, a younger brother of Henry, Earl Northumberland in the 1390s. Thomas served as chamberlain and then steward of the royal household and was a successful former soldier and diplomat, for which service he was created Earl of Worcester by Richard II in 1397. His castle at Wressle is first mentioned in 1403 when he was executed and forfeited for his part in the rebellion of that year against Henry IV. The son of his nephew Hotspur Percy was eventually restored to the earldom of Northumberland, but Wressle was only restored to the Percies in 1469 when Edward IV restored the 4th Earl to his honours after several years' captivity in the Tower of London. He was killed by a mob at Topcliffe in 1489. The 5th Earl particularly favoured Wressle and the fine furnishings and fittings which survived in the south range until it was gutted by fire in 1796 probably dated from his period. He also built the bakehouse which still survives. The 6th Earl died in poverty in 1537, having left his estates to the Crown since he was childless and his brothers were disgraced for their part in the recent Pilgrimage of Grace rebellion. Thomas, nephew of the 6th Earl was restored as 7th Earl of Northumberland by Queen Mary in 1557. He was later executed by Elizabeth I for rebellion. His successor died a prisoner in the Tower of London and the 9th Earl was also incarcerated there, and his cousin Thomas was one of the instigators of the Gunpowder Plot of 1605 against James I. The earldom finally became extinct with the death of the 11th Earl at Turin in 1670, but a junior branch of the family retained possession until the 19th century. After most of the palace was dismantled in 1650 the south range remained occupied by tenants until the fire of 1796. See page 111.

Wressle Castle   *Wressle Castle*

Wressle Castle

Although embattled and surrounded by a moat, Wressle was a palace rather than a fortress, the outer walls being only 1.2m thick and pierced with large windows. From a drawing of it made c1600 the arrangement and appearance of the destroyed parts is quite clear. It had four ranges set around a court about 25m square and four corner towers, the eastern ones being about 10m square and the western ones rectangles about 10m wide by 14.5m long. Each tower had latrines in projections where the ranges adjoined, and a stair turret rising above the corner facing the court. A tall five storey gatehouse with a lofty outer arch and a NW stair turret lay in the middle of the east range, which was 6m wide internally and contained three storeys of rooms used by servants and officials under the command of the constable, whose rooms lay in the NE tower. Beyond this side was an outer court with mostly timber framed buildings. The great hall occupied the upper storey of the west range, which was 10m internally. The dais at the south end had its own huge fireplace, and there was also a hearth in the middle of the floor, with a louvre in the low-pitched roof above. The kitchen lay in the NW tower and the room added by the 5th Earl lay in the adjacent NW corner of the court. Although described as a bakehouse, the ruins, now heavily overgrown, suggest it was actually some sort of porch, perhaps with a stair.

The southern towers and the range between them, 7.5m wide internally, now gutted, but with the ashlar masonry almost intact, contained private apartments with windows of two lights with an unusually thick mullion and transom. A doorway near the east end of the north wall led from steps up from the court into a lobby at the end of the private hall or presence chamber. This room has two large windows on each side, with a fireplace between those on the south. From here there was access into a chapel in the SE tower, the interior of which has been patched up with brick. There was also access from this lobby to three other chambers, one over the lobby and two in the upper levels of the tower. Below the private hall were the kitchen, buttery and pantry which served it, these lower rooms having a number of inserted late 16th century windows in the outer wall. At the other end of the private hall was a private chamber, then a lobby (over which was another chamber) with access through to the main hall and the withdrawing room in the SW tower, and a timber stair down to the offices and servants rooms below. The withdrawing room, 12m long by 7.5m wide, had a latrine in the NW corner, a fireplace in the SE corner and three windows, one of them originally a fine oriel. Because of the height of this room the SW tower contained only three storeys, the top room being the lord's bedroom, although the other towers each had four storeys, two of them above the roofs of the main ranges.

YAFFORTH: HOWE HILL   SE 347950

This castle was probably built during the 1140s to control a ford over the River Wiske. A document of Richard I's reign referring to the castle in the past tense suggests it was destroyed by Henry II either on his accession in 1154, or after the rebellion of 1173-4. A ditched motte 4.5m high and 23m across on top stands on a low hill, originally an island, beside the river.

YARM CASTLE   NZ 419126

Nothing remains of a castle on the west bank of the Tees near the town centre. There is mention of the place-name Castledyke in the 13th century and Castle Close is mentioned in the 16th century.

YORK CASTLE   SE 605515   E

William I subjugated the fortified city of York by building two motte and bailey castles on either side of the River Ouse. One castle was erected in 1068 and the other seems to have been added a few months later after an attack on the first one. When a Danish fleet arrived late in 1069 and the local populace rose to support the invaders, the castle garrisons set alight to neighbouring houses to give themselves a clear field of fire. In the confusion the fire spread throughout much of the city and the castles were captured and destroyed. William rebuilt both castles, a house being destroyed as a result of an extension to one of them. The castle on the east bank was the stronger of the two, with the Ouse on one side and a lake created by damming the River Foss on the other, the motte filling most of the remaining side. This castle was burnt down in 1190 when the local Jews were allowed to take refuge in the wooden keep and were besieged by the townsfolk.

York Castle: interior of Clifford's Tower

York: Interior of Multangular Tower

Corner tower of York Castle   *Clifford's Tower, York Castle*

Rebuilding in stone of some of the buildings of the castle on the east bank began during King John's reign but the defences seem to have remained mostly of wood until Henry III, on a visit to York in 1244, ordered a rebuilding in stone. Over £2,450 was spent during the next twenty years on the construction of a curtain wall with two gatehouses, at least three circular flanking towers, two halls, a chapel, kitchen and prison, plus the keep known as Clifford's Tower on the heightened motte. Although the water defences strengthened the castle they also caused problems. Flooding in 1315 weakened the curtain wall on the SW side, necessitating a series of buttresses being built there in 1326. The castle was garrisoned against the Scots in 1319. A tower, probably the keep, was repaired to house Queen Isabella in 1327, and in 1333 Queen Philippa was provided with an exchequer on the north side of the bailey. The Countess of Buchan was allowed to use the keep in 1338 whilst her husband was serving with the king in France. In the 1360s Edward III spent £800 on repairs after a report describing the keep as cracked in two places because of subsidence of the motte and the hall as ruinous since timber from its tiled roof had been taken to repair the dam. The gatehouse and one of the towers had also suffered subsidence, causing cracks to their vaults. Perhaps because of the state of the buildings the king when visiting York tended to stay in the Franciscan Friary. The castle was more of a depot and prison than a residence, the keep housing the royal treasury on several occasions, whilst there was a mint in the bailey until it moved into the buildings of the former hospital of St Leonard in 1546.

In 1484 Richard III had some of the castle dismantled prior to rebuilding but his defeat and death in 1485 prevented any work being executed. The castle was described as ruinous in the 1530s but £40 was spent on repairs in 1556 and the county justices collected money in the 1580s for repairs to the gatehouse, bridge and Moot Hall. In 1596 the gaoler Robert Redhead began demolishing parts of the castle. After he had unroofed the keep the work was stopped after a strong protest by the city council. From about this time the keep became known as Clifford's Tower on account of that family, by then Earls of Cumberland, being hereditary captains of the castle. The 5th Earl garrisoned the castle for Charles I, and in January 1643 it was manned by 200 men under Colonel Sir John Cobb, Clifford's Tower being re-roofed to take cannon and a new drawbridge being built over the moat at the foot of the motte. The city surrendered to Parliament after a siege following the Royalist defeat at Naseby in the summer of 1644. Damage done to Clifford's Tower during the siege was repaired, and it remained garrisoned during the 1650s, but it was gutted by an explosion in 1684 and then remained roofless. In the bailey an older building was remodelled to provide a new Grand Jury House in 1667-8 at a cost of £133, and the common hall was repaired in 1670 and totally rebuilt in 1674 at a cost of £650.

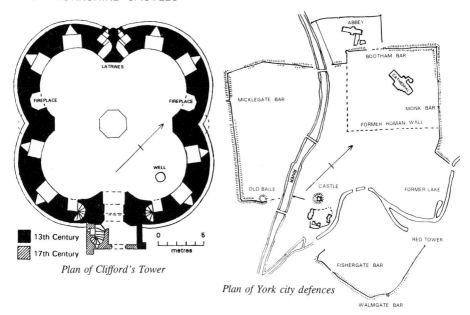

Plan of Clifford's Tower

Plan of York city defences

The cathedral lies just north of the centre of the Roman fortress which measured 490m by 420m. The Multangular Tower at the west corner of this rectangle represented a 4th century strengthening of the original 2nd century wall which had timber towers projecting internally at the corners and at intervals along the sides. The bastion measures 13.5m in diameter over walls 1.5m thick and had a crosswall to support an upper floor. The ashlar-faced upper parts with arrow-loops are 13th century. Not far north of it is a tiny Saxon tower projecting internally and containing a vault, a rare survival of a Saxon secular structure of stone. By extensions towards the banks of the rivers Foss and Ouse the city more than doubled its size from that enclosed by the Roman walls. The Vikings covered the Roman walls with a huge bank, and eventually the suburbs which developed west of the Ouse and SE of the bridge over the Foss were also given substantial ramparts. The main gates were rebuilt in stone in the 12th century and strengthened and adorned with bartizans and barbicans in the 14th century. All four of them retain portcullises. The wall itself stands on the older rampart and is quite low for much of the 4.5km long circuit, most of which has survived. It is of various periods from the mid 13th century onwards, and includes much 19th and 20th century repairwork. There are forty towers, the earlier ones being semi-circular and the later ones rectangular. Almost all of them have been reduced to the level of the main wall-walk and parapet.

The western castle site, known as the Old Baile, lies at the SE end of the suburb west of the Ouse. Damming of the Foss produced a lake 100m wide from which water flowed into the moats around the motte and the north and west sides of the bailey of the eastern castle. These moats were partly severed on the east side by the mid 18th century and were dry by c1800. The city walls were manned during the 1745 Jacobite rebellion, although they were not regarded as defensible against the cannon of that age, and the munitions in the city did not include any artillery. In 1800 the city council resolved to demolish the walls. Luckily this was not carried out, although the next thirty years saw some small breaches of the walls and the removal of most of the barbicans of the gateways as a serious hindrance to traffic.

The bailey of the stone castle measured 105m by 90m and was enclosed by a wall 2m thick still standing 7.5m high on the SE side, together with a round tower 8m in diameter at the south corner and a second tower of more modest size and projection further east. Each tower contains a room with three arrow-loops with shouldered arches to the embrasures. In the SE tower the loops are cruciform and there are two more on an upper level. A patch in the wall beyond the second tower marks the site of a third tower. Between the surviving towers is the drawbridge pit of a former gatehouse which had two flanking towers each about 5m wide. Old drawings suggest that these towers had three storeys, were about 12m high and were linked high up by an arch. The gateway was blocked c1600 and demolished in 1735. Backing onto these remains is the Debtors's Prison of 1705. More fragments of the curtain survive behind the Female Prison of 1780 on the NE side of the bailey, where there were once two more flanking towers, whilst the Assize Courts of 1777 stand astride of the line of the SW curtain wall. The twin towered main gatehouse facing north towards the city centre survived until the early 19th century. A length of the city wall extended from the west bank of the motte ditch to the River Ouse, but the eastern part, including the Castlegate Postern, was demolished in 1826.

Clifford's Tower is formed of four interlocked lobes 13m in diameter over walls 2.5m thick above a battered plinth, producing a quatrefoil measuring about 21m across and 9m high to the wall-walk. Circular turrets are corbelled out above the re-entrant angles. Such a squat building is not a tower in the true sense of the word and it is best regarded as an usual form of shell keep which instead of having inward-looking lean-to rooms was entirely roofed over with beams supported on a central octagonal pier. Each lobe has two embrasures on each of two storeys. All of them had arrow loops, but the upper ones had windows above the loops. The east lobe contains a well. This lobe and the south lobes each contain a stair to the upper storey and wall-walk and on the lower storey probably formed one room, into which led the entrance passage, which has a portcullis groove and a rebate for doors. The other lobes have fireplaces and latrines and although poorly lighted must have been habitable rooms divided off with timber screens. The upper storey was probably similarly divided into a hall with two chambers divided off in the north and west lobes. At this level there is a tiny chapel in a forebuilding projecting in front of the entrance. The arcading on one side of the chapel would have been obscured by the portcullis when it was raised. This forebuilding was mostly rebuilt after the Civil War and bears the arms of Charles II and the Cliffords. A third storey which originally housed the portcullis windlass was not replaced in the rebuilding.

York: Saxon tower on city wall

Fishergate Bar at York

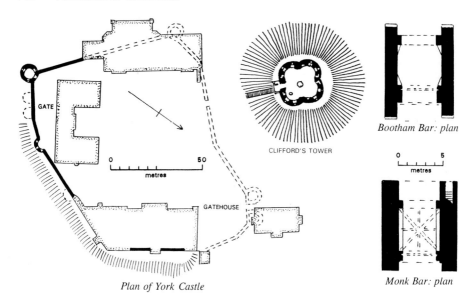

CLIFFORD'S TOWER

Plan of York Castle

Bootham Bar: plan

Monk Bar: plan

The castle on the west bank of the river later passed to the archbishops, probably when Geoffrey Plantagenet was both Archbishop and Sheriff of York. It had evidently ceased to be used as a fortress capable of independent defence by 1322 when the citizens agreed to help defend the new palisade provided by Archbishop Melton around this part of the city should it come under attack. Soon afterwards the SE and SW sides of the bailey were walled in stone as part of the city wall. At the south corner is the Bitchdaughter Tower. Quarrels between the townsfolk and the archbishop over defence of this quarter continued until the 1450s when the mayor and corporation took possession of it. Being an open space, normally used for grazing, it was used for musters, boys as young as 7 being required to attend with a bow and arrows along with all men up to the age of 40. A prison built in the north part of the bailey in 1802-7 was closed in 1868 and demolished in 1880. The bailey has since been built over and the northern ramparts of the bailey obliterated. Not far beyond their site is the Victorian Bar, a new gate in the city wall created in 1838. The section of wall between the motte and the river was demolished for a road in 1878.

From the south corner of the Old Baile the city wall runs almost straight for 500m to meet Micklegate Bar, a gatehouse with a Norman arch with a portcullis groove behind it and 14th century round bartizans. It is 8m wide and projected 7m beyond the walls. An extra passage was made here in 1731. The 15m long barbican was demolished in 1826 leaving just the former shoulder-lintelled doorways to its wall-walk. There were posterns on each side of the barbican. Like all the other gatehouses except one this gatehouse has two gunports in the topmost storey where a pair out of the twelve guns purchased in 1511 were mounted. Another 120m beyond Micklegate Bar the wall has a sharp angle at Tofts Tower and then heads back towards the River Ouse. The section opposite the station has the wall-walk carried over on three modern arches. A tower at a corner midway to the river has three cross-loops with roundels on the arms. By the river are the North Street postern, near which are a series of 17th century musket loops, and the circular Barker Tower, with a conical roof. Chains were slung across the river to the Lendal Tower on the north bank, which was originally similar in form.

York. Barker Tower   *Walmgate Bar at York*

The Lendal Tower lies only 100m from the section of Roman wall running NW to the Multangular Tower. Only the first half of the wall between there and Bootham Bar survives. West of this section lay St Mary's abbey, the precinct of which was in the 14th century provided with its own embattled wall with several turrets in addition to the Water Tower on the river bank, St Mary's Tower at the north corner, and the rectangular Postern Tower about 40m in front of Bootham Bar. These walls have only a very narrow wall-walk and the crenels in the parapet were closed with shutters. Bootham Bar is about 7.5m square, with 14th century bartizans with small figures on the parapets. The side towards the city with further bartizans on the corners was rebuilt in 1719 and again in 1832, when the barbican on the outside was removed.

The two straight sections of the city wall running round behind the cathedral from Bootham Bar to Monk Bar stand on Roman footings. The Robin Hood Tower at the corner is essentially a 19th century structure. The barbican of Monk Bar was demolished in 1825 and an extra passage was then created beside the 8m square gatehouse, which mostly projects within the line of the walls. The passageway and the room above are vaulted and there are figures on the parapet. A straight stair leads up in the NW wall. In the third storey the portcullis machinery still survives. The wall then runs past the footings of the east corner tower of the Roman fortress, makes a re-entrant angle at New Tower and then runs 100m to meet the River Foss. Parts of this section are built with arcading below the wall-walk. A rectangular tower and the Laverthorpe Postern beside the river were demolished in 1829.

The 400m gap as far as the Red Tower was originally a wide fishpond made by damming the River Foss and required no other defence. The Red Tower is a 16th century structure of brick with a hipped roof and a latrine projection. About 300m beyond it lies Walmgate Bar, the only gateway still retaining its 14th century barbican, which is 16m long and has side buttresses at the outer corners, on which are bartizans. There are bartizans on the outer corners of the gatehouse itself, which retains a portcullis. This gateway, which measures 7m by 8m, suffered some damage in the siege of 1644, especially to the iron gates that had been fitted in the barbican by 1630. The gatehouse has a timber-framed inner part on Tuscan columns added c1580. The wall then runs SW to a corner and then west to Fishergate Bar, now just an archway, but originally a gatehouse with two rectangular towers. This whole section was rebuilt in 1502. At about 80m west of Fishergate Bar the wall turns through a corner at a tower in which is an equal-armed cross-loop, and then runs north to the rectangular Fishergate Tower built in 1505, beside which was a postern closed by a portcullis. The tower measures 8.5m by 6.5m. The 100m gap between here and the castle was originally filled by the damming up of the River Foss.

GLOSSARY OF TERMS

ASHLAR - Masonry of blocks with even faces and square edges. BAILEY - defensible space enclosed by a wall or a palisade and ditch. BARBICAN - Small walled court of modest defensive strength. BARTIZAN - A turret corbelled out at the top of a wall, often at a corner. BASTION - A projection no higher than the curtain wall. BERM - A narrow strip of land between a wall and a ditch. BLOCKHOUSE - Building containing guns commanding an estuary or river. BRATTICE - A covered wooden gallery at the summit of a wall for defending its base. CORBEL - A projecting wooden bracket supporting other stonework or timbers. CURTAIN WALL - A high enclosing wall around a bailey. FMBATTLED - provided with a parapet with indentations (crenellations). ENCIENTE - An enclosing stone wall. FOUR-CENTRED-ARCH - An arch drawn with four compass points, two on each side. GEORGIAN - The period of the reigns of George I through to George IV i.e. 1714-1830. JAMB - A side of a doorway, window or opening. KEEP - A citadel or ultimate strongpoint. The term is not medieval and such towers were then called donjons. LIGHT - A compartment of a window. LOOP - A small opening to admit light or for the discharge of missiles. MACHICOLATION - A slot for dropping or firing missiles at assailants. MERLONS - The upstanding portions of a parapet. MOAT - A defensive ditch, water filled or dry. MOTTE - A steep sided flat-topped mound, partly or wholly man-made. ORIEL - A bow window projecting out from just the upper part of a wall. PARAPET - A wall for protection at any sudden drop. PELE or PEEL - Originally a palisaded court, later coming to mean a bastle or tower house. PLINTH - The projecting base of a wall. It may be battered (sloped) or stepped. PORTCULLIS - A wooden gate made to rise and fall in vertical grooves. POSTERN - A back entrance or lesser gateway. RINGWORK - An embanked enclosure of more modest size than a bailey, generally bigger but less high than a motte summit. SALLYPORT - Secret means of leaving a fortress for foraging or counter-attacking. SHELL KEEP - A small stone walled court built upon a motte or ringwork. SOLAR - A private living room for the lord and his family. STRONGHOUSE - Dwelling made difficult to break into but not equipped for an active defence against a sustained or determined attack. TIERCERON VAULT - Vault using secondary ribs as well as primary ones. TOWER HOUSE - Self contained defensible house with the main rooms stacked vertically. TUSCAN - One of the Greek architectural styles. WALL-WALK - A walkway on top of a wall, always protected by a parapet. WARD - A stone walled defensive enclosure.

The Red Tower, York

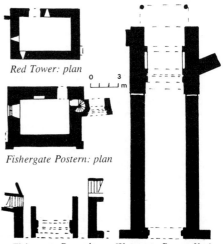

Red Tower: plan

Fishergate Postern: plan

Fishergate Bar: plan   *Walmgate Bar at York*